CORPORATE PUNISHMENT

Smashing the management clichés for leaders in a new world

James Adonis

JOSSEY-BASS
A Wiley Imprint
www.josseybass.com

First published 2010 by Jossey-Bass
A Wiley imprint
www.josseybass.com

John Wiley & Sons Australia, Ltd
42 McDougall Street, Milton Qld 4064

Office also in Melbourne

Typeset in ITC Giovanni LT 10.8/13.8pt

© James Adonis 2010

The moral rights of the author have been asserted

National Library of Australia Cataloguing-in-Publication entry:

Author:	Adonis, James, 1979–
Title:	Corporate punishment: smashing the management clichés for leaders in a new world / James Adonis.
ISBN:	9781742169866 (pbk.)
Notes:	Includes index.
Subjects:	Management.
Dewey Number:	658

Cover design by Xou Creative

Cover image © stock.xchng/Michelini

Lyrics adapted from: "I WILL SURVIVE" (F. Perren/D. Fekaris) © Bibo Music Publ. Inc./ Perren-Vibes Music, Inc. Licensed courtesy of Universal Music Publishing Group

'Rudd unfazed by poll slump', first published by *Lateline*, 19 May 2009, is reproduced by permission of the Australian Broadcasting Corporation and ABC Online. © 2009 ABC. All rights reserved.

Printed in China by Printplus Limited

10 9 8 7 6 5 4 3 2 1

Contents

To Greg Loveday

Thank you for being the most incredible business partner, an infinite source of wisdom and a true inspiration.

About the author

© *Gaye Gerard <www.gayegerard.com>*

James Adonis is one of Australia's most well-known people-management thought leaders. He is a leading international expert on employee engagement and the co-founder and Managing Director of Team Leaders, a company dedicated to developing and recruiting the best front-line managers.

By the time he was 24 James was managing a team of 100. His major achievements have included taking a team that had employee turnover exceeding 70 per cent and reducing it to zero where it was maintained for two years. He has also achieved employee engagement results that have exceeded not only the industry standard, but world's best practice.

The author of three books and a nationally syndicated blogger with the Fairfax group of online news sites, James's original thoughts are read by tens of thousands of managers and business owners every week.

Thought-provoking and entertaining, James's keynote presentations and workshops show companies how to solve staff turnover, engage all generations and win the war for talent. James has presented to audiences on almost every continent and in almost every industry, and has an impressive list of clients, including McDonald's, Ernst & Young, American Express, Coca-Cola and Gucci.

James can be contacted at <www.jamesadonis.com> and <www.teamleaders.com.au>.

Acknowledgements

The greatest support I had while writing this book came from my loving and authentic best friend, 'Spooner'.

She was the cure whenever I had writer's block, my compass when I felt lost and always the one to turn up like magic when I craved company. A profoundly inspiring speaker, wickedly funny intellect and the most brilliant writer I know, Oonagh masterfully adds colour and vibrancy to everything and everyone she comes into contact with (a verb hereby known as 'to oonerise').

For more information on this dazzling woman and her work, please visit Oonagh's website <www.oonagh.tv>.

Introduction

Starting from scratch

If I had a dollar for every time I heard a manager use a tired and old cliché, I'd be over the moon. Somewhere along the line, managers have gone from speaking in clichés to speaking in circles. Sometimes it's hard to tell the difference.

I love the looks on managers' faces whenever they blurt out one of these cringe-worthy clichés. Their eyes light up, their lips transform into a proud smile and they sit back expectantly, waiting for their wisdom to sink in. They patiently loiter until they've witnessed your positive reaction to their profound words of wisdom; until they've savoured it and tasted it. And once they notice your appreciation, they're as happy as Larry; they're grateful you are the recipient of this selfless goodness. No, not just the recipient, but the *beneficiary* of their worldliness.

It's hard to pinpoint the real victims in this sorry saga — the ones who fall between the cracks. Perhaps it's the employees who are forced to listen to this drivel, unable to respond with a wail of '*whatever*' since, as the subordinate workers, their hands are tied in obedience and faked reverence. Instead the faithful followers resign themselves to being content with a roll of the eyes and a mumble once their manager's back is turned, accepting that this is all in a day's work.

Or are the victims really the managers themselves? In their earnest attempts to look good and sound professional, all they end up doing is showcasing their lazy vocabulary and unimaginative minds. They become infected with the same sameness and predictable predictability all sufferers of this cliché syndrome endure. Instead of being inspiring, they become irritating. Instead of being looked up to, they look untoward. Instead of being the cream of the crop, they become like a bull in a china shop, butchering honest and frank conversation.

To make matters worse, of course, is that many of these clichés are blatantly untrue. But they've been bandied about mercilessly by a throng of managers for so long now they're established as gospel. In a nutshell, that's really what this book is all about. I've asked hundreds of people for the most over-used clichés they've heard and I've ripped these clichés to shreds in this book. It's not just an exposé of the management clichés poisoning the beautiful English language. It's also a stripping of each cliché down to its naked truth. It's a revelation of how the opposite of the cliché is usually what's most accurate and appropriate. At the end of the day, this book is a protest, a movement, a changing of the guard. What we need is a breath of fresh air and this book is a start.

I guess this is all easier said than done. Even as you've read this introduction, you would have noticed it's been littered with clichés. And I use the word *littered* intentionally, since that is what a cliché is. Litter, garbage, scraps. You have my word that it ends here. The rest of this book avoids them like the plague.

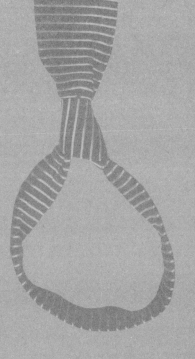

Part I

Full team ahead

Chapter 1

There's no 'I' in 'team'

I was bullied throughout high school for being gay. At the time I could never understand why. Sure, I would sit on the sidelines reading *Woman's Day* magazines while the boys played soccer, and yes, I'd pretend I was injured so I could secretly study the sealed section of *Cosmopolitan* — but I didn't feel I was overtly girly. A consequence of being tagged with the gay hairbrush was that I would never be picked for team sports. So while the captains of each team chose their players, I would always be the last one standing, left with nothing to do but accept the expression of indignation splashed across the snarled and scrunched-up face of the captain who was unlucky enough to be lumped with the 'friend of Dorothy'. 'I hate this as much as you do', I would mumble, as I reluctantly packed away my half-finished crossword puzzle and headed frazzled towards the football field.

This, I believe, was the beginning of my aversion to working in teams. It was a bitter scar and a brittle start that would only worsen when I entered college where I encountered the dreadful world of group assignments. It was here I realised there is most definitely an 'I' in 'team'. I did most of the work, and I would go berserk when others would shirk their responsibilities and cause us to miss deadlines. And it was I who would get irked by the lack of enthusiasm evident in my teammates, who would express more gusto at a funeral than with the project at hand.

This brings us to the business world where, if this cliché were a person, it would be an exhausted and exasperated little bugger, dragged from training room to meeting room, teaching employees that as individuals they are not as important as the collective team, which in effect is what socialism is all about. The reason why socialism is an idealistic experiment that fails miserably in every country in which it's tested is that it doesn't embrace the palette of human behaviours such as desires and dreams and diversity. It abandons the progress that's borne from competition. It darkens the vibrancy that emanates from creativity. And it sucks the soul out of any setting by promoting to people that their individual needs and style are of lesser importance than the team's. Yes, that's what socialism does. It turns people into communist versions of Prince Charles and Camilla Parker-Bowles — beige people trying to fit in to a certain family and a specific way of being.

Libertarianism is the solution in whatever exciting and daring way it's masochistically manifested. When you shove an 'I' in 'team' you acknowledge that effort is not equal. Some people will pull their weight while others will wait to be pulled. Some people will take the initiative while others will initiate the taking. Some people will rise to a challenge while others will challenge a rise in workload. Effort in a team is never equally spread among the doers — and when you profess there is no 'I' in 'team', you're less likely to notice those who are genuinely carrying the team to glory. The result is that rewards and incentives aren't discriminated towards those that deserve them.

Try telling Michael Jordan there's no 'I' in 'team'. His illustrious slam dunks, incredibly high jumps and prolific point-scoring trumped the competition and led the Chicago Bulls to win three consecutive NBA championships — and then some. Could the Bulls have achieved such stellar success without their superstar Jordan? Not a chance. And it's not just his immediate team who would have suffered, but the NBA as a whole. There's no doubt there would have been a drought of interest in basketball had Jordan chosen a different sport to pursue; for instance, wife-carrying — an actual sport in Finland where male competitors race each other while carrying a woman on their shoulders. The fallacy of this chapter's cliché is evident in every team-based sport that relies on a star player, something that is eerily similar to the working world where one or two star employees are usually the engines of a team's success.

The greatest psyched-up hype of this past decade has been the generation Y phenomenon. I must confess that I've dabbled in it and have babbled on about it throughout various phases of my career. There are times when I've been an ardent believer of generational differences and other times where I see far more similarities than contrasts. Mostly, the former have coincided with occasions where I've needed money. I now know that one of the most dangerous things managers do is manage by generation. They treat gen Ys the way HR gurus tell them to treat gen Ys. They communicate with Baby Boomers in the way a management consultant tells them to communicate with Baby Boomers. And the outcome is they disengage the gen Ys who act like Boomers and the Boomers who act like gen Ys. I would now like to totally eradicate the need for any more work or research to be done on generation Y, or even the upcoming generation Z by stating the obvious: *manage by individual, not by generation*. This means having an intricate understanding of the values and drivers of each individual employee. Not of the generation. Not of the team. But of the person. That's what amplifies true engagement.

There isn't just one 'I' in 'team', but several, often many. The best teams are those that are built around all of those 'I's; where each 'I' understands the others' communication styles, work preferences, strengths and weaknesses. You might be thinking, 'I can't believe he used the word *weaknesses*. That's so 1980s'. Yes, I could have used the politically correct 'limitations' or the softer 'blind spots', but I feel the word 'weaknesses' forces us to be brutally honest with ourselves. It's such a harsh word and there's really nothing wrong with admitting that you suck at stuff. For example, I will never be a good singer, no matter how much I crave to perform on stage at a Carols by Candlelight concert. I choose to accept my singing as a weakness, a big weakness ... and move on.

For those who crave to stand up and stand out, think big and act big, there will always be a big fat 'I' in 'team'.

Chapter 2

Together everyone achieves more

There are some activities I dislike doing on my own. The cinema is one. I love the flicks but I'd rather give them the flick than go by myself. Shopping is another. I much prefer to have the company of friends when I venture into a shopping centre. And let's add kissing to the list, because that's usually more pleasurable when someone else is involved. But work, I'm afraid, doesn't work as well. When I'm asked to join a team, I shudder at the thought of who my teammates and leader are going to be and I clutter my mind with apprehension of what's to come. This occurs not because I disagree that teams are brilliant, but because they're occasionally overrated. Teams are luminous in some situations and ominous in others. As the acronym suggests, they often *do* achieve more — but they also frequently achieve less.

The 'together everyone achieves more' cliché requires greater analysis on the word 'more'. Collectively, yes, it's possible that a team's progress can be accelerated, but what also happens is that the productivity of the individuals within that team *decreases* as the group gets bigger. This was proven in a tug-of-war experiment by an engineering professor called Max Ringelmann. His research initially involved getting people to pull a big rope on their own while he measured the strength of each individual's pull. He then got them to pull the rope again — only this time they were to do so in groups. He was astounded to find that the total strength of the group's pull was in fact *less* than the sum of the individuals' solitary pulls, and that as the groups expanded in size, the team members' individual output continued to decline.

Here's a personal example. There are few things in the world that I loathe more than moving furniture. There was one time in particular when I lived with a flatmate and we decided to swap rooms. She moved her furniture across without a whimper or a hint of worry. I, on the other hand, hired a removalist just to take my bed from one bedroom to the other. It's shameful, I know. To my dismay, when the removalists arrived, they asked me to give them a hand, so I stood up and gave them a round of applause. To my disdain, their version of 'give them a hand' didn't mean a standing ovation but a request for manual assistance. They were asking me to engage in blue-collar activity when the only blue collar I'd ever worn was to a fancy-dress party. Regardless, I reluctantly obliged. I exerted more effort in moving my pillows than I did helping those guys move my bed — but it wasn't intentional. When I committed to helping them out, I was genuinely all in, yet when push came to shove (so to speak), I barely stressed a muscle. You might look at that scenario and conclude the strength of three men is what resulted in less exertion on my behalf. Or you can look at the Ringelmann Effect as well as countless other reputable studies that have shown there's an automatic reduction in individual productivity (even in white-collar environments) when people are forced to work with others in teams.

Here's a useful question to ask: is a team *really* needed for this project? There'll be many times when the answer is a resounding 'yes', in which case go for it. But there'll be occasions when upon asking yourself that question you'll realise, no, the setting up of a team could actually be counterproductive. It could be that people working on their own are far more likely to produce a better outcome than if they were to work in tandem with others.

You can see this play out in what is the biggest waste of space known to humankind: the committee. For some reason, committees attract people who need to be committed, not to a task but to an asylum. Several years ago I served on the committee of a well-known not-for-profit association. I saw things during those 12 months I thought only ever happened on *Dynasty*. It was as if Alexis Carrington was right there in the boardroom saying slanderous sentences such as, 'Take this junk, and your blonde tramp, and get out of my house!' and 'I'm glad to see that your father had your teeth fixed … if not your tongue'. From catfights to catnaps and from handcuffs to handicaps, this committee injected the funk into dysfunctional. It, like many others, was incredibly talented at *not* making decisions and at absolving itself of any accountability. It was a disorganised, irrelevant and unnecessary mess. We would have been better off had the leader allocated us our duties and managed us remotely. It proved to me once and for all that dictatorships are the most efficient form of leadership. That's why you need to evaluate the 'Is a team really needed for this project?' question. The planning and plotting, the brainstorming and decision-making, the conflict resolution and team dynamics all consume precious resources.

One hazard of teams is groupthink. The more cohesive a group of employees, the greater the chances will be of them thinking in consensus, resulting in crushed creativity. If you've ever caught yourself saying something like, 'It was a really good idea at the time', don't be surprised if it's teamwork that initiated and encouraged the bad idea. Fashion is the most obvious example of groupthink. Scores of people around the world follow a fashionable trend for no other reason than to be just like other people they consider as hip. Even if you look at today's fashions, you can see adults blindly adhering to fashion statements they'll look back on in five years' time and cringe, such as women wearing sunglasses so big it looks like they've got eyeballs larger than their cheeks, or men whose shoes are so pointy it seems like they've only got one toe — the middle one. In 2020, they'll check out old photos of themselves and say, 'What was I thinking?!' And that's the problem — they weren't.

It's important for me to point out I'm not against teams. My entire business is all about educating managers on how to manage them for maximum mileage. I am, however, critical of this cliché since it implies that together everyone *always* achieves more, which is simply not the case. Nevertheless, the teams who do achieve more do so not just because they're in a team, but because they're led by an excellent leader. Cabaret dancers don't perform tremendously just because they're in a troupe. A talented choreographer takes the lead. Olympic rowers don't win races just because they're in a team of four. A coach guides them to victory. Some leaders, even when lumped with a team who isn't achieving more, are able to turn it around. Other leaders are also able to turn it around … 180 degrees.

In many workplace situations, a more suitable acronym for TEAM is Teamwork Echoes Absolute Madness.

Chapter 3

Singing from the same song/hymn sheet

There's a lot to like about the pretty city of Salisbury. Located in the United Kingdom and with a population of just 50 000, it's only a stone's throw away from Stonehenge, it's home to the majestic Salisbury Cathedral and, most importantly, it achieved notoriety in 2008 when its town hall staff were banned from using the phrase, 'Singing from the same hymn sheet'. If only every other city sang from the same hymn sheet. The term 'hymn' is often interchanged with the word 'song', which is what I'll be using for the rest of this chapter. No matter which words you use, the objective of this cliché is still the same, and that is to silence differing opinions in a group by expressing a united view publicly. Diversity used to be about race, gender, and other minorities, but maybe it's time for a look at the outspoken and the unspoken, too.

This cliché is the reason clichés exist. Employees, keen to 'sing from the same song sheet', surrender their vocabulary to the corporate slaughterhouse where it gets butchered and manufactured into slabs of verbal meat without a lot of backbone. You're a walking contradiction if you: (a) believe in this cliché but hate clichés or (b) hate this cliché but use others in your lexicon. It's because there's such an emphasis on singing from the same song sheet that clichés have now permeated the corporate world. As Stephen Fry has said, 'It is a cliché that most clichés are true, but then like most clichés, that cliché is untrue'. Confused? That makes two of us.

There's a dark side to singing from the same song sheet. Sure, the words in that little phrase sound innocent and harmless, but they disguise a tyrant's tirade. When managers cajole their employees to 'sing it loud, sing it clear, sing it my way in my ear', there's an implied *forced compliance*, which is to say managers want their employees *saying* the same thing even if they don't *think* the same thing. Surely a better school of management would be *influenced compliance*, where the aim is to still get employees saying the same thing but doing so because they actually agree with it. I had a manager who would issue the most implausible instructions, so before complying I would impulsively question why. The response would always be a sharp 'Because I've asked you to, James — *that's why*', before fixing her stare on me as if she had missiles shooting out of her eyes and she didn't want to miss my skull. Her method of forced compliance is the same one that singing from the same song sheet is all about. It's the 'agree with me, or else' strategy where intimidation is the first and last resort.

To sing from the same song sheet stinks of being inauthentic and stings of disingenuousness. I like to call it the Milli Vanilli factor. This is the infamous pop duo who released a string of successful albums, only to be revealed they were lip-synching the whole time. The Milli Vanilli factor can be seen in politics, where politicians publicly support their beleaguered leader while behind the scenes they're plunging the knife deeply into their boss's back. The Milli Vanilli factor can be seen in courtrooms, where lawyers defend the indefensible knowing the person they're representing is guilty rather than innocent. The Milli Vanilli factor can be seen in the corporate world, where a client of mine is working for an organisation that's undergoing both a merger and a restructure. The CEO, in his attempts to quell tension in the office, has banned all staff from talking about the upheaval. In order to get thousands of employees to 'sing from the same song sheet', he's stopped them from talking altogether so that gossip and rumour are immediately stopped. So now he's got an entire building full of people putting on a front, acting in a way that goes against their true beliefs. Yes, the silly Milli Vanilli factor is still spilling around corporate corridors. But if you discourage dissent in favour of people singing from the same song sheet, you're not entirely blameless.

There's no denying the degree to which dissension is frowned upon. Having a critical or analytical employee within the team is one of the best ways to avoid groupthink, because it could be that everyone else is singing the wrong song, and the staff member refusing to join the corporate choir is in fact the one humming the right tune. I understand why so many managers diss the dissenters. Quite frankly, they're annoying; they create a lot more work in the short-term, and they nit-pick everything. I had one in my team a long time ago and I couldn't stand him. Whenever I'd see him walking towards my desk, I'd be tempted to call security. Whenever he'd open his mouth, my gut instinct was to start throwing things in like those laughing clowns at fun fairs that turn their heads from left to right as punters insert balls in their gaping jaws.

Everything he had to say was a criticism or a suggestion for improvement. But not once did I try to silence him. I always listened, kept an open mind and took his advice on many occasions. I didn't try to make him sing from the same song sheet. His role in the team, no matter how frustrating, was necessary. It's usually the most talented people who are the greatest dissenters, yet managers incorrectly associate dissent with disloyalty.

There are some exceptions. If you're pitching to a potential client, it's important to deliver a consistent message, and if you're in the middle of a business negotiation, it's essential those on your side, are on your side. But in the majority of cases, singing from the same song sheet is about as dull as toast with no butter and as dull as butter with no toast. Thankfully, history is full of social and political movements that were pioneered by dissenters who made the world a better place as a result of speaking out.

The feminist movement in the '60s and '70s was led by women who refused to sing from the same unequal song sheet. The protest movement against the Vietnam War was led by people who refused to sing from the same military song sheet. From the civil rights movement to the gay rights movement, and from the environmental movement to the anti-management-cliché movement, all of them sparked change not by staying silent and agreeing with the masses, but by speaking out. And they made sure they were heard.

Singing from the same song sheet has never been so out of tune. It's time for a remix.

Part II

Strut your staff

Chapter 4

Employees are our greatest asset

Type into Google the search term 'employees are our greatest asset' and up will come more than 2.9 million pages of management sages prophesising the value of employees and how vital they are to an organisation. In reality, all we have to do is look at the recent global financial crisis to see how easily and quickly these 'assets' were dispensed, left incensed and with barely a few cents as a redundancy payout. When the market's hot, employees are the equivalent of mail-order brides: employers will pay whatever it takes to have the right talent hanging off their arms. But when the market's massacred, employees go from being the greatest assets to the greatest asses as they're forced to join the unemployment queue.

Employees aren't assets. After dedicating my career to the importance of employee engagement, you might think this is a contradiction, akin to the Dalai Lama joining the Ku Klux Klan, but it's true. Employees are no more an asset to your company than your customers. The core definition of an asset is something of value that you *own*. You don't own your employees. Even the term 'employee' in itself is arbitrary, because everyone who works for you is really self-employed whether they know it or not, and whether they like it or not. Sure, you might pay them a regular wage and take up all of their working hours, but fundamentally they are sole traders choosing to contract out their services to one client (you) in return for a fee (salary). You don't own them, which means they're not an asset. Stalkers own people, not managers. If when you call their phone you just sit there breathing down the line, then fine, perhaps your employees are assets. But for the rest of you who don't rummage through your employees' garbage, the people in your team are self-employed contractors.

This cliché presumes *all* employees are assets. You only have to be a manager for a day to discover many of them are liabilities. Some hold you back while others attack just because you give them some feedback. Some are slack while others are more notable for what they lack, such as brains. Yes, it's noble to think everyone has untapped talents that need to be mined, but that doesn't take away from the fact there'll inevitably be people in your employ who'll be more of a hindrance than a help. They have facets of evil, not assets of marvel.

The real asset is the *relationship* between you and your employees. This is what's strengthened when you show appreciation, and this is what's destroyed when you lack care and understanding. It's the subtle difference between working with a replaceable resource and working with a colleague you trust. It's the confluence of mutual consideration and respect when two people are connected purposefully at work. The fact that one is hierarchically subordinate to the other is irrelevant. All that matters is that the two parties have a bond, which even if not a 'Come over to my place to drink beer and play Twister' kind of bond, is still a bona fide bond nonetheless.

Employees are more *risks* than assets. They'll make you look really good or really bad. They'll fill you with joy or fill you with ire. They'll have you loving your job or praying for a demotion. In effect, people management and risk management are intertwined. A common notion in the world of risk management is that there are four main ways to treat a risk. You can *avoid* it. You can *reduce* it. You can *retain* it. Or you can *transfer* it. The same principles apply to the world of people management.

You can *avoid* the risk of employees by not having any, or if you're lumped with them regardless, you can ignore them. One of my client's employees adored the HR lady because she was the only person who'd talk to him during the day — even though he sat in an intimate space with three colleagues and his manager.

You can *reduce* the risk of employees by recognising that employee engagement should be every manager's first priority. I was presenting to a board of directors recently and when I got to the part about the importance of building relationships with employees, a gentleman sitting next to the chairman sincerely asked if it was possible to hire someone to do this task, and I quote, 'Obviously a woman'. It wouldn't have been so disturbing if the other board members hadn't nodded in agreement. I could see each of them pondering, 'Now, why didn't *I* think of that?'

You can *retain* the risk of employees by accepting that the potential benefit of a terrific employee outweighs the potential negative impact of a terrible one. For our American readers, 'terrible one' would exclude the 50 or so employees who commit worker-to-worker homicides in the United States each year, as well as the 140 000 others who victimise their colleagues in more creative ways.

You can *transfer* the risk of employees by outsourcing them to other companies, managers and the world wide web. Growing aggressively are websites such as <www.guru.com> and <www.elance.com> which enable anyone to engage a freelancer wherever there's an internet connection. I've had a lot of my graphic design requirements fulfilled by people I've never met in countries I've never visited.

My psychic says there's no such thing as a coincidence, so I was shocked to stumble across a page in the latest issue of Australia's leading business magazine with the ground-breaking headline of 'Employees are your greatest asset'. I'm going to humour them for a few seconds and assume this statement is true. After all, it's used by some executives even more frequently than 'moving forward'. If senior managers believe so fervently employees really are their greatest asset, why do so few of them walk the talk? They're willing to pay lip service to it but when it comes to getting down and dirty, they desist. The convenience of cost-cutting surpasses the consequence of low morale. The 'I'm so important' walk down the corridor beats the open-door policy they espouse. To quote a similarly over-used cliché but a dissimilarly true one, actions speak louder than words.

A computer can't just walk away from an owner it doesn't like. A piece of real estate can't give its buyer the silent treatment. A printing machine can't tarnish the reputation of its user all over town. Unlike assets, employees always can.

Chapter 5

Management is not a popularity contest

Most people want to be popular—even if they don't admit it or know it. That's why people love dogs so much. The devotion they receive from a puppy makes them feel wanted, needed, popular. They figure that if they can't rely on a human to chase them and lick their face, they may as well let a dog do it. Oscar Wilde once said, 'The only thing worse than being talked about is not being talked about'. And it's true. When it comes to managing a team, your level of popularity can boost your success. There's no need to push it away, put it aside, or pull it apart.

I'd like to introduce you to two managers. One of them is called Awful and the other is named Cheerful. They're both identical, with the same experience, the same qualifications and the same decisions. However, both of them adopt very different ways of being. Awful is the kind of person who makes a Somali pirate look like Shirley Temple. He yells rather than tells, puts down more than he lifts up, makes people happy only when he leaves and should be prohibited from breeding. Cheerful, on the other hand, is the kind of person who genuinely loves people. She asks rather than demands, cares more than she scares and energises people with her laugh. Which one of the two would be able to get employees to do more? In the short term, the answer is both. Awful's menacing manner alarms employees into giving him more, while Cheerful's dedicated demeanour disarms employees into giving their all. But that's just in the short term. In the long term, Awful's tactics are unsustainable. People get burnt out, they rebel, they resign. Cheerful's employees remain loyal, lively and hardworking. When people like you, they'll do anything for you.

The science behind why people follow a leader is aptly known as 'followership'. Employees choose whether or not to follow you, and they make that choice every day. The words you impart, the tone you take and the body language you project, all influence that choice. A little while ago, I was on a flight back home from an interstate conference. I happened to be the first one to get off the plane. Now, I know Sydney airport really well since I spend more time there than in my own place, but my mind was jaded that evening. Upon alighting from the plane, instead of turning left to head towards the exit, I turned right. But when I turned right, I was so sure it was the correct way, I walked with such confidence, such conviction, such resoluteness, that *everyone* followed me towards the right. Despite there being a plethora of bright green exit signs and plenty of arrows directing people towards the baggage carousel, a huge mass of people followed me until we reached a dead end and were left scratching our heads wondering what went wrong.

In fact, it's not what went wrong but what went right. What went right was followership. People want to be led, but if I'd stood there and shrieked at them like a trumpet with teeth, it's unlikely they would have turned right. They would have questioned me, analysed their surroundings and double-checked. Instead, they blindly followed and when they realised what they'd done, they humbly chuckled. The difference between the two options is huge, but the distinction is small. And that distinction is what popularity represents. When you get one person on side, and then another and then another, before you know it, everyone's following you, and not because they have to, but because they want to.

Being a popular leader doesn't mean that you make popular decisions. But it does mean when you're popular, employees are more likely to hear and adhere to your decisions even if they inherently disagree with them. You can see this in the way you respond to your friends. I've got mates for whom I'd do absolutely anything. They could ask me to help them move house, and despite preferring to chew on razor blades, I would grumble but assist. But then I've got other friends for whom I'm not as eager to cooperate with, even though I enjoy spending time with them. They could ask me to clean the dishes after they've cooked me a delightful dinner, and I'd probably reply with, 'Pardon, je ne parle pas l'anglais. Vous parlez francais?' I bet you're the same. You'd happily do the unthinkable for some people in your life, but for others you just won't go there. The reason why this occurs is not because of you but because of them — the messengers. People are more likely to comply with an instruction when they've got belief in the messenger. This belief might consist of various elements that are important to them personally, such as honesty, competence, reputation, trust and likeability, to name but a few, all of which form part of the overall theme of popularity.

What's the deal with Bill Clinton? Here's a man who embarrassingly cheated on his wife in the Oval Office, and yet by the time his second presidential term ended, his popularity rating was sky-high. And what's the deal with Sarah Palin? Here's a woman who says things such as, 'There is hope and opportunity in our neighbouring country of Afghanistan' and couldn't name in an interview a single newspaper she's ever read ('All of 'em, any of 'em that have been in front of me over all these years' — *there are more than 1400 American newspapers*), and yet she was credited for energising John McCain's presidential campaign. The commonality between the two is *charisma*. It's that undefinable quality that's hard to teach and difficult to develop, but the two of them have it in abundance to such a degree that their millions of supporters merrily ignore their indiscretions and lack of judgement. Their charm fuels their popularity, their magnetism inspires their followers and their electric nature charges up people to listen to what they say, even if what they say is banal and irrelevant. Could Clinton or Palin have achieved that level of public adoration without the popularity their charisma gave them? Unlikely.

When I put it to you that management is most certainly a popularity contest, that doesn't mean everyone in your team should love you. It's rare to win them all over. Some will hate your guts no matter what you do. I reckon I was a popular manager, and yet there was a time when I received vicious death threats from someone who sounded remarkably like a soon-to-be-fired employee threatening to shoot me in the foyer of my apartment building, which would have been an interesting experience since my building doesn't have a foyer.

The word 'popularity' comes from the Latin *popularis*, which means 'belonging to the people'. And really, that's what management is all about.

Chapter 6

Employees resist change

If there's just one cliché that's responsible more so than any other for keeping millions of millionaire consultants in business, it would have to be this one. Managers find that getting employees to embrace change is like asking them to change gender, and so the first conclusion they jump to is that employees are resistant to change, when they're really not resistant at all. Employees love change, evidence of which can be seen by how quickly they initiate it in their personal lives. They're happy to move house, which is akin to having your teeth pulled out by a tractor, and yet if you get them to change desks at work they'll hyperventilate. People are quick to adapt to new technologies such as smart-phones and iPods, yet try to introduce a new computer system and they'll act like it's a violation of their human rights. The same applies with other big changes such as getting married, having kids, losing weight, plus many others, all of which prove that people are not resistant to change. But when they're confronted by it at work, they hate it. The common denominator isn't the employee, but the workplace.

When people react negatively to change at work, it's only because they've been burnt too many times by managers with little concern for how the change will affect their staff. Employees aren't resistant to begin with, but they begin to display resistant behaviours when their expectations are broken. I worked for a corporation that went through a major merger, resulting in a line that separated the Good Old Days from the Bad New Days. The Good Old Days were characterised by fun, friendship and freedom to sensibly spend money. The Bad New Days were about as pleasant as a head massage from Freddy Krueger. Cost-cutting became the new black as line items were blacked out from managers' budgets. Regardless, we remained agreeable. We accepted the changes that came our way. When salary increases were frozen, we understood. When training days were culled, we understood. When the monthly social nights were canned, we understood. We weren't resistant to any of those changes… until they cancelled the Monday morning delivery of fruit. That was when we got angry. We just couldn't believe out of all the areas to hack, they attacked the inexpensive apples and mandarins. It was as if we'd given them our loyalty but all we got back was a lemon. Well, now we were sour, so we rebelled. We'd call in sick, complain ceaselessly and reduce our productivity. The managers observing our behaviour would have said we were resistant to change, when in fact we were fine with it up until the point where their level of disregard for us overtook the need for change. It wasn't the change that was the problem, but the overzealousness of our managers.

People don't resist change. But they do resist being changed. Arranged marriages are a prime example of this. When someone is forced to get married they're *being changed*, which is why so many women resist it. But when people get married because they're deeply in love with each other, then they're swimming along with the *flow of change*. The gulf between the two is enormous. One makes you feel like you've got influence over what's happening, while the other gives you no choice whatsoever.

I worked in a contact centre where half of the employees were service assistants and the other half worked in sales. The senior management team introduced a new rule requiring the service assistants to up-sell to all customers. In management's mind, this was a simple change in process, but to the service assistants this wasn't a change in process, but a change in character. Service people and sales people are two very different personalities. We had demure and gentle souls who were perfect in service roles, but couldn't get pushy with a wheelbarrow let alone a customer. All of a sudden, they were supposed to 'close the sale' and 'overcome objections' when all they wanted to close was the phone and the only objections they had were their own. Asking service people to sell was like asking me to fix your car engine trouble. All you'd get back is a 'say what?' with a shake of the head like a *Jerry Springer* guest. 'Oh no you didn't, oh no you didn't!' The result was a flood of resignations, plummeting productivity, unhappy customers and disengagement that made *The Exorcist* look like *Driving Miss Daisy*. What they were resisting wasn't the change, but the idea of being changed.

It's human nature for us to run away from pain and head towards pleasure. When employees react badly to change at work, it's because the fondness they have for the present state (pleasure) blocks them from embracing the proposed change (pain) even when the change is better than the status quo. You can see this in attention-seekers. The pain they're running away from is the anguish of not being noticed, so they'll head towards the pleasure of popularity by doing things they think will impress others. They tell bad jokes that are as amusing as a carjacking; they talk with loud voices like a high-pitched car alarm going off in the office; and they make up stories, like an ex-colleague of mine who had us believing for three months she had a terminal illness, when in fact the periods she was having off work weren't for surgery but for job interviews. When someone points out to an attention-seeker the pain they're causing themselves is greater than the pain of just being who they are, that's when their behaviour starts to change. Likewise, to get employees to embrace change, arouse the underlying dissatisfaction with their present state. Rather than focusing on the change itself, highlight the pain that already exists. Create a case for change before imposing it, because they're not resistant to change; they just have a soft spot for what they've already got.

Part of the problem that causes perceived employee resistance is that managers expect it to happen. They believe employees are going to push back whenever a change is introduced, and so this inevitably becomes a reality. To pre-empt the resistance, they encourage and cajole people to accept change, and instead of avoiding the resistance, they end up creating it.

I had an employee who was a big Maori football player twice my size. He would call in sick at least once a week, and almost always on a Monday. It got to the point where I'd say to him on Fridays, 'Okay, see you on Tuesday!' He'd always bring in a doctor's certificate verifying the viruses that would interrupt his life. One day I was flicking through all of the certificates he'd given me, and I noticed many anomalies. There were spelling mistakes (such as 'physitian' instead of 'physician'), different signatures (even though the same doctor's name appeared on each one) and phone numbers that had nine or seven digits instead of eight. After further investigation, I discovered that all of these doctor's certificates were fakes, so I had to sack him. I was really nervous because I expected resistance to the change I was about to enforce on his life, plus, he was a martial arts black belt while the only black belt I held was a DKNY one I'd purchased the weekend before. So sure was I of his upcoming resistance I had a security guard standing outside the meeting room just in case he tried to throw a punch. In the end, the sacking was fine. The tension was still there, but he didn't resist. He didn't throw a punch, just a little spittle, but I think that was a speech impediment. I remember being so relieved the security guard was present because I was certain it would have turned ugly.

A few weeks later, I was walking down a dark alley in the middle of the night near my apartment building, and who should come walking towards me but the big Maori rugby player. I started saying my prayers. This was the end. I'd been tracked down and now I was about to be knocked down. But, no, we had a cordial conversation as if nothing had ever happened. In fact, he'd recently moved into the area and now we were neighbours, so there were several more joyful encounters in the following months, each time without a hint of resentment that I was the one who terminated his employment while an armed guard watched on. I knew at that moment all of the resistance and tension I'd felt during the firing process wasn't in him, but in me. I'd caused it. He was okay with it.

I can recall very few employees who were resistant to change just for the sake of resisting it. The vast majority embrace progress, so long as they don't feel like they're being short-changed by their employer.

Chapter 7

People don't leave jobs, they leave managers

What I love most about my ex-managers is the 'ex' part. Most of them have been complete idiots. I tell you this so you don't think I'm only opposing this cliché because I've been blessed with brilliant bosses. It's not the case. Besides two who spring to mind, the rest have taught me what not to do. I've been bullied and bowled over, blamed and framed and shamed in public and yet I still hung around these dropkicks like a scarecrow doing more crowing than scaring. I know I sound bitter and I *hate, hate, hate* sounding bitter because really I'm not bitter at all. Okay, maybe just a little. The point is this: most employees don't leave managers. Some do, of course, but the majority have other reasons.

The main distinction I'd like to make is that employees leave for reasons *controllable* by managers. This means they don't necessarily leave because *of* their manager; rather, they resign for factors their manager has influence over. This isn't just playing with words. I've been to events where I've heard experts tell an audience of managers that they're the cause of their employee resignations, and I always feel sorry for these supervisors, especially the ones who are genuinely good at heart, but who just happen to be experiencing high rates of staff turnover. By stating sentences like, 'People don't leave jobs, they leave managers', you're attacking the person, not the behaviour. The default response people hold when you attack their character is one of defence, which doesn't help the situation.

When I was in my early 20s, I hired a driving instructor to teach me how to drive a manual car. He furiously cancelled the lesson halfway through, grabbed control of the vehicle and drove me back home where he yelled at my dad, 'Your son drives like a bloody kangaroo!' and sped off. Fair enough, I almost killed the guy on three occasions and I'm pretty sure I destroyed his clutch, but his heated response has meant that 10 years later I still haven't sat behind the wheel of a manual car. So, when you start saying irresponsible throwaway lines such as, 'People don't leave jobs, they leave managers', you're putting at risk the self-esteem of managers who mean well but just aren't aware of the hidden factors that influence employee retention. Factors such as the major elements of intrinsic motivation, the essential steps to high staff engagement, the path to building meaningful relationships, plus a range of other facts and factors to do with communication, career development, coaching and performance.

Last year I surveyed 2400 employees to find out what it is they hated the most at work. The results of the survey garnered a lot of media attention because what everyone expected to come out at number one got outnumbered.

The primary aspect of work that employees despise more than any other isn't their manager but their colleagues. In fact, their colleagues came out several times in the top 10 and many times throughout the top 50. At number one was 'lazy and underperforming colleagues', at number five was 'negativity', at number seven 'annoying and inconsiderate coworkers', at number eight 'lack of teamwork', at number nine 'gossip and backstabbing' and on it went. The question they were asked was, 'What gets you angry, upset and frustrated at work?' As one respondent so eloquently put it, 'My colleague has a voice like fingernails on a chalkboard. She speaks to me, and everyone, as if we're children and not quite bright. She reminds us regularly that she has a Master's degree or a degree in this or that to make her point. She stares at me from odd places in the room, and watches what I'm doing. She magnifies her every ailment, coughing very loud with her mouth wide open, or sneezes with a huge "*Achooo*" and if you say, "Bless you", she's off and running again about all her ailments. She's negative about everything. She always eats in my office and she smacks and slurps and stares at me'. And another respondent was a little more succinct with what she hated the most at work: 'The troll that sits three desks up from me that thinks she knows everything'. Employees often feel the greatest angst not against their bosses but against their buddies sitting right next to them.

In many instances, employees resign because it's just time to go. It's not the manager's fault or the organisation's fault. Blame doesn't need to be apportioned. It's just that employees outgrow their role, or the company can't cater for every career goal, or maybe they're going travelling solo, or who knows what else. To say, 'Employees don't leave jobs, they leave managers' ignores the reality that employees get itchy feet. All managers can do is make the farewell experience special enough so if employees feel comfortable coming back, they can. It's a bit like moving out of home. You might love your parents dearly, but the time will come when being 40 and sleeping in the spare room isn't cool — even if you're Italian. If at that point you move out, will people blame your parents and say they're incompetent for not holding on to you? Unlikely. They'll understand it was simply time for you to move on.

Of course, lots of employees resign directly because of their managers — but this cliché doesn't say, 'Some people leave jobs, others leave managers'. It's quite frank in its assessment when it boasts, 'People don't leave jobs, they leave managers', explicitly expressing that managers are responsible for every resignation. An interesting question that arises is this: is an employee more likely to *leave* a *bad* manager or is an employee more likely to *stay* with a *great* manager? I haven't come across any studies that compare the two, but I'd comfortably take a guess and say the latter. Employees can tolerate a bad manager but they latch on to a great one. In my work, I speak to hundreds of employees and managers each year, and I hear an endless number of stories from people who *have* an awful manager, but not very many talk about when they *had* an awful manager, which implies maybe they just put up with it.

One of my ex-managers was a workplace bully and I was his victim. He was a vile and vindictive piece of work. He put the error into terror and the evil into devilish. It was as if his position description had 'Torment James' scrawled across the top of it. My deepest fantasy is that he's reading this right now, recognising himself in these words. (If you're asking yourself the question, 'Is he talking about me?' then yes, it probably is you, you rotten scoundrel.) His unspoken mission was for me to resign. Knowing this, I refused to give him the satisfaction of seeing me hand in my resignation letter, and so it began — the contest, or rather, the battle, to see who would quit first. He knew I wanted him gone. I knew he wanted me gone. And so for two years I dug my heels in, putting up with his daily dose of derisory remarks, his scheming gaze and conniving ways. Finally, he announced the news that made me more ecstatic than a naughty dalliance in a nightclub. He was resigning — and with that, I had won the game. It felt like I'd been on a series of *Survivor*, even though to most it appeared like we were playing Trivial Pursuit, with emphasis on the word 'trivial'. Regardless, I'd emerged victorious despite the scars I'd endured over the previous 24 months. I was the last man standing and that's all that mattered. I hadn't quit even though my boss was a monster — and most managers aren't that malicious. When there's a big enough reason to stay, people can tolerate a bad boss.

So does this mean managers can get away with being anything less than brilliant? No, because there are huge differences in productivity when employees are energetically engaged as opposed to scarcely satisfied. There are also great gains in loyalty when managers build relationships rather than shallow conversations; and there are pronounced profit increases when employees are developed from being competent performers into talented stars. It takes an amazing manager to do these things, and I firmly believe most people are capable of achieving managerial excellence. Others, like my ex-boss, are robbing a village somewhere of an idiot.

The cliché 'People don't leave jobs, they leave managers' leaves a lot to be desired.

Chapter 8

My way or the highway

Think back to when you were a kid and you asked a parent or a teacher or someone else in authority, 'Why?' It might have been in response to an order to go to bed, a demand to do your homework, or as was the case with me, it was a reaction to being told to stop wearing women's clothing in kindergarten. If you were like many kids, a common answer to your question 'Why?' would have been a stern, 'Because I said so'. Unless you were particularly obedient, most kids, I found, would find some way to rebel against this retort. Instead of going to bed, for example, I would hide behind a wall so I could still see the adults-only television my folks were watching. And instead of doing homework, I would write stories, usually based on what I'd watched the night before on the adults-only TV. 'Because I said so' is the equivalent of 'My way or the highway'. The first instinct for employees is to respond in the same way kids do when they hear that lazy remark. Their negative reaction becomes less about your way and more about 'No way'.

This cliché is fraught with friction from the very beginning because it sizzles up straight away an adversarial relationship between the leadership team and its employees. It's a 'You're with us or against us' mentality. It's the 'Do it or else' direction. One of my earliest jobs was in retail while I was a teenager. It was a cheap and nasty manchester store, and it really taught me the vital life skills of folding towels and doily appreciation. We had a manager who'd approach us while we were at the cash register and demand we give him money from the till. The amounts varied from $50 to $400, and because he was our boss and the requests were accompanied not by a question mark but by a full stop, we had no choice but to hand over the cash. He'd then leave the store for a couple of hours, come back, ask for more money, depart once again, and so on. Tension boiled up and suspicions arose. All of this created the 'us-and-them' divide that supplements the 'My way or the highway' mode of managing. And it wasn't long before a group of us surreptitiously followed him to see where he was going, only to be stunned he was gambling away the money on the races. He subsequently got sacked. I know we wouldn't have been so eager to follow him had he adopted a different management style. Our primary motivation wasn't concern for the business, but revenge at an inflexible ogre. When you engage with the 'My way or the highway' approach, you're immediately putting offside a team of people who will seize the first opportunity they can to put you in your place.

A critical component of competent managers is buy-in, which is when they get their employees on side before implementing any sudden changes. An element of buy-in is when you outline the rationale and benefits as to why your employees should be avid advocates as opposed to reluctant minions. The 'My way or the highway' cliché is devoid of these explanations. It deems them to be unnecessary since the dictatorial manager's decision is final. It's the equivalent of being sent to jail without a reason why. There's a lot the prison system has in common with the corporate world. Some countries have death sentences; management clichés are death sentences. Prisoners attend disciplinary hearings; employees attend performance appraisals. Courts issue restraining orders; managers issue restraining orders whenever they imply 'My way or the highway'.

A real risk of this cliché is your employees will do precisely as you say. They'll be so conscious of the repercussions if they were to disobey you, even if they did see something inherently wrong with your decisions, they'd be too scared to speak up. It's the workplace equivalent of *The Emperor's New Clothes*. For those unfamiliar with the classic story, it's about the vain emperor of an affluent kingdom who cared more about wearing stylish clothes than he did about anything else. Two conmen acting as tailors promised to make him the most splendid suit from an exquisite cloth that was invisible to people who were either stupid or incompetent. The emperor believed them, and when they finally 'dressed' him in his new suit, he pretended to see it so that nobody thought he was a fool. Even the emperor's servants were too afraid to speak their minds, fearful they'd be exposed as hopeless for not being able to see his clothes. The emperor went on a ceremonial parade through the streets of the kingdom because the people had heard of this invisible suit and they wanted to see which of their neighbours and relatives were ignorant or inept. As the emperor's procession made its way past the crowd, the townsfolk lied and said, 'Look at the emperor's magnificent new clothes', 'They're so beautiful' and other comments to hide their disappointment. Everyone was now acting as if they could see the emperor's new clothes, until a young child who had no job and could see things only as they were, cried out, 'The emperor is naked!' This murmur spread very quickly throughout the crowd, and before too long all of the bystanders had caught on to the fact the emperor was indeed in the nude. The emperor realised the people were right but he couldn't admit it, so he continued with the parade pretending he was wearing invisible clothes.

At work, you need to ask yourself whether you're an employer like the emperor, where the illusion of consent is more important than the reality. If this is the path you choose, the danger you're riding into is that even if your employees instinctively know your vision is destined for failure, they'll obligingly comply like the obedient robots you want them to be — just like the emperor's 'loyal' servants. But in the end, you'll be the one caught with your pants down.

One of the fastest ways to kill morale is via the 'My way or the highway' modality. To deny your employees the opportunity to contribute their comments or to discuss and debate your decisions will drain them of the motivation they need to obey your wishes. It's like driving a car without knowing you've got a flat tyre, which incidentally, happened to me last year. In hindsight, I should have realised it sooner because of the unusually high number of vehicles beeping their horns and flashing their lights over the previous three days. I just assumed they were compliments. Eventually, a big, burly, beefy truck driver yelled out of his window, 'You've got a bloody flat tyre, mate. You're gonna kill someone!' So I stopped the car and saw he was right. It wasn't just that I had a flat tyre, but that there wasn't much of a tyre left at all. I called the roadside assistance hotline and the friendly operator asked me if I had a spare one in the boot. 'No', I replied. 'In that case', she said, 'the car will need to be towed'. My parents' place was close by so I called my dad. 'What do you mean you don't have a spare tyre?' he bellowed. 'Have you checked the boot?' 'Yes', I answered. 'Check again', he ordered, which I did before confirming there definitely wasn't a tyre in the boot. 'Do you mean to tell me that *my son* hasn't got a spare tyre in his car?' Um ... 'Have you tried lifting the cover?' he asked. What cover? There's a cover? And lo and behold, unbeknown to my ignorant self, upon lifting the cover in the boot, I saw there was a spare tyre waiting to be used.

Here's the lesson: your employees and their suggestions are represented by the hidden car tyre. The cover is whatever's blocking you from accessing what they have to say. It's the veil of pride or the shroud of ego or the curtain of busyness that's stopping you from being interested enough in a fundamental element of your team's success. The flat tyre is represented by the unfortunate consequence of a flat team, flat innovation and flatlining results. And then there's you left stranded, like me, scratching your head, wondering how you could have possibly missed it.

'My way or the highway' is ultimately an ultimatum. Mediocre employees will choose your way since their choices are limited, but your most talented people will get off at the next exit, eager to escape your micromanagement as fast as they can. Unless they get freedom to think, scope to influence decisions and latitude to flex their initiative, they'll choose the highway every time.

I once had a job working in one of Australia's finest dining establishments. It was an odd job because all I did was take plates of food from the kitchen to the waiter who would then take the dishes to the patrons. If there were ever a job that required fewer brain cells than a mailbox, this would be it. The kitchen was only a few metres away from the waiters' stand, so if they simply stretched their arms far enough, they'd be able to grab the plates themselves. Instead, they had me and five others standing in the kitchen doing nothing for 40 minutes waiting for our turn to take a plate to a waiter, and then repeating that 40-minute process on and on throughout the night. The evening would painfully drag on even slower than movies that win the Academy Award for Best Picture. My endless and earnest suggestions on how to better utilise me as a worker fell on deaf ears. Their response was a curt 'My way or the highway', which was like telling me to go on, now go, walk out the door, just turn around now, 'cause you're not welcome anymore. They thought they'd be the one who'd hurt me with goodbye, they thought I'd crumble, they thought I'd lay down and die. Unsurprisingly, that restaurant has since closed down.

Arrogance. That's the characteristic at the heart of this cliché. It might work for you as a quick short-term solution, such as in a crisis or an emergency, but it's not sustainable for long-term engagement and productivity. If you're a perpetrator of this phrase, it's arrogance that makes you think you've got all the great ideas, but don't mistake arrogance for confidence. As Peter Mcintyre elegantly described, 'Confidence comes not from always being right but from not fearing to be wrong'. People who are arrogant, on the other hand, are best described by Benjamin Franklin, 'People who are wrapped up in themselves make small packages'.

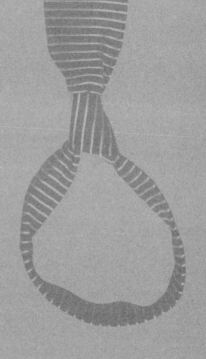

Part III

Business as unusual

Chapter 9

Work on the business, not in the business

Have you ever met a business book consultant? He or she can often be found hanging out at seminars with colleagues such as business book trainers and business book speakers. These are the people who regurgitate information they've read in a business book, or worse, in a summary of a business book they've perused online. It's easy to spot them in a crowd. Just listen very carefully for the person whose vocabulary includes common phrases that are found in bestsellers, usually from the 1970s. If you have the misfortune of engaging one of these people in conversation, or rather, in a book reading, you'll inevitably see this ripper of a cliché lusciously revealed from their well-read lips. Repeated incessantly to insouciant small business owners, the 'work on your business, not in your business' cliché is frequently prefixed with, 'The secret is to …' Newsflash: it's not a secret. It stopped being a secret when Michael Gerber unveiled it in his fairytale-style book. That was over two decades ago.

Let me make it clear there is nothing wrong with working in your business. If your company has grown because you love selling and are great at it, then continue selling. If your floristry business has expanded because there's nothing you enjoy more than putting together beautiful bouquets, then continue with your flower flamboyance. If your auto-mechanic business has boomed because you're good with cars, don't switch off the ignition to what drives your passion. Happiness in business comes not from building an empire, but from doing what you adore. Those who entice you to work 'on' your business forget that maybe you're not cut out to be a general manager. Perhaps you weren't put on this earth to think strategically. And you do not have to build a franchise if your home business is fulfilling your every need. It's because of this 'working on your business' cliché we have so many technically competent entrepreneurs becoming leaders when the last thing they should be doing is having any contact with people. They should be holding a paintbrush, not a performance appraisal. They should be hammering a wall, not an employee. They should be grooming a dog, not a successor.

Sometimes you have no choice but to work in the business. For example, when you're in the start-up phase and you have less money than a wannabe actor, someone has to sweep the floors, serve the customers and settle the invoices. Whenever there's a crisis that needs fixing, the one person who knows the business inside out needs to come from the outside in to fix it. When I first started my company, I was equipped with two metaphorical bags. One was a handbag of $30 000 that represented my life's savings. The other was a sandbag of the 'Work on your business, not in your business' way of thinking. Within six weeks, the bag of cash was slashed to nothing because I had spent all of my money outsourcing everything — and I do mean *everything* — including my writing. In the very early days I would get a ghostwriter to pen my articles even though authorship is what I love the most and is by far my best skill. (If you're painfully persevering with this book like a starving artist looking for inspiration, you might disagree with that latter point.) Nonetheless, my point is I am much more fulfilled now where I joyfully work in my business doing work I find irresistible, than to be living life off a business plan.

One of the best ways of connecting with your employees is by working in the business. Experience what they experience and handle what they handle. Politicians are masters at working 'on' the business of governing the country while knowing they'll only win votes when they work 'in' the business of governing the country. That's why you see them throwing a football for the cameras when the only thing they've thrown in the past is a tantrum. This is why you'll see them reading to kindergarten kids when the only thing they're interested in reading is the latest opinion poll. And this is why you'll see them donning a hard-hat at a construction site when the only thing they've ever put on their head is a bandaid. Working *in* the business makes you more relatable.

Spending too much time *on* the business can distract you from what's really going on. There are early warning signs that start to brew in a business, which when left unbridled, boil into bigger problems. The early warning sign of staff dis-engagement can turn into high attrition. Archaic processes can turn into administrative nightmares. Customer indiff-erence can turn into declining revenues. It's difficult to notice early warning signs when you're deluged with strategy and engulfed by your BHAG (big hairy audacious goal), which is yet another one of those business book terms I bet has been enthusiastically thrust upon you at some stage in your career. Unsurprisingly, it's an acronym.

There's probably a whole other book I could write just on the overused nature of acronyms. From SMART goals to a SWOT analysis, and SME to FMCG, granted, they make it easier to communicate long titles. My gripe is with those experts who somehow, miraculously, are able to get the perfect solution to fit into an acronym of the problem they're trying to solve, such as a change consultant whose formula for change management just happens to be CHANGE, or a sales coach whose five-step process for getting more sales has the amazing coincidence of fitting into SALES. Are they for REAL (rudimentary experts and losers)?

I'm not suggesting you shouldn't work *on* your business. And I'm not suggesting you should work entirely *in* your business. All I'm saying is it might be a mistake to neglect one of the two like an ageing relative without an estate. You need a bit of both — a balance. The corporate world is infested and infected with idiot managers who were wonderfully effective at working *in* the business ... until they got promoted. And now that they're working *on* the business ... they suck at it. Or vice versa. Some people are magnificent at the managing and disastrous at the doing. To be adept at one could put you out of depth on the other. But to master both would be ideal. To switch between the two would be perfect.

The next time someone talks to me about the E-Myth, I'm just going to assume they've got a lisp. What they're trying to say are the more apt terms like amiss or remiss. Regardless, for this section, class is dismissed.

Chapter 10

It's nothing personal, just business

Despite being a city boy living in Australia's most densely populated suburb, I have huge admiration for the countryside and its wide-open plains, its vibrant terrains and its community feel where everyone knows your name. It also scares the hell out of me. Life without a 24-hour convenience store within five metres of my building is too unbearable to even think about. Opening my apartment window to the sound of birds cheeping rather than car horns beeping would freak me out. And the thought of neighbours saying hello as they pass me on the street would, quite frankly, be creepy. Yet even as a lover of all things loud and fast, I do mourn the demise of heart and soul in business. To a certain degree it's still alive in the countryside, and that's what I adore the most when I visit, but as those regional towns get more populated and pop-cultured, they're bound to follow the sad and sorrowful chant of the city corporate types who harmonise that it's nothing personal, just business.

Relationships are at the core of business. Whether it's between managers and their employees or representatives and their customers, the one common element that weaves throughout business is trust, and trust is determined by the strength of a relationship. It's widely accepted people don't buy from those they dislike and distrust. Evidence of this can be seen in the horrifying field of cold-call telesales. Organisations think it's perfectly okay to disturb someone in the privacy of their own home late in the evening to sell them anything from home loans to hotel rooms.

I used to be one of those irritable and intrusive people. I would call residents to sell them financial advice, or sometimes I'd be paid to survey them on sensitive topics like their prostate issues. Unfortunately for my eardrum, my calls were usually conducted while they were having dinner, halfway through their favourite TV show or fighting with their spouse, so I'd get abused and accused and eventually hung up on. Of course, I would always get my revenge. I'd call them back with a scowl of 'As I was saying…' or if they were especially nasty I'd ring them back and whisper the word 'cow' when they answered — irrespective of whether they were male or female. Though I must admit, I would have much preferred to shout it rather than whisper it, but I had to be careful not to be heard by the boss. Regardless, what I learnt was that in the absence of a trusting relation-ship, it's nigh on impossible to conduct any business. It's very personal.

Just like some of the other clichés that have been exposed in this book, this one similarly tries to make you choose one option over the other. What the orators of 'It's nothing personal, just business' don't realise is that business *is* personal — there's no separating the two. People look at companies, especially big corporates, as machines or creatures or giants or monoliths that are tough to crack and rough to break into. People talk about large corporate organisations as if they have a life of their own, unable to be conquered. Small business owners say throwaway lines like 'It's so hard to enter the corporate market' as if they're trying to sell bikinis and ham to the Taliban in exchange for a sensual foot massage. They forget these blue-chip beasts are full of people just like them. Confident, insecure, smart, dumb, happy, moody, young, old, fat, skinny, divorced, married, ugly, pretty, funny, serious, caring, arrogant, lonely, loving individuals with their own hang-ups and aspirations. It's not a cold-hearted company making a decision, but an individual or individuals with feelings and emotions. Business is very personal.

If it really is nothing personal, then personality wouldn't be so important in a business transaction. When you see a bit of yourself in a salesperson and you like what you see, or if they make you laugh and it makes the vibe less icy, you're connecting on personality. Instead, in the corporate world, people try to blend in. Rather than standing out by showing more of who they really are, they fade out by glowing less than they otherwise could. They put up a façade that, in their attempt to disguise what disgusts and repeal what repulses, ends up hiding their magnificence as they merge into the abyss of being just like everyone else.

I was ensnared in this cage when I first started my business. I was one of those try-hards who thought the corporate market was something that had to be 'cracked', so my marketing materials had a photo of me wearing a tie (when

I would have preferred to place my head through a burning window), my hair combed down (when at the time I tended to wear it up like Whitney Houston) and accompanying text that sounded like a doctoral thesis (when my natural style, some would say, is camper than a ballet dancer's tights). A wise mentor eventually gave me some seasoned advice, and so I took off the tie, unbuttoned my shirt, funked up my hair and wrote copy incorporating the language and attitude I'd use with my friends. My business turned around because I'd stopped making it about business, and instead, made it personal.

This heartless cliché fools people into thinking emotions can be isolated from a business outcome. It can't be done. If what you're doing affects the wellbeing of others, then business is personal. If the work you do has an effect on the energy and atmosphere of your workplace, then it's personal. If your actions and words make people feel worried or harried, glad or bad, bored or deplored, then you cannot avoid the obvious fact that business is very, very personal, no matter how much awful news you deliver with this cliché as the disclaimer. To do otherwise is to be missing the essential leadership ingredient of emotional intelligence. Some people force themselves to keep business separate from any kind of feeling, and so they experience a greater range of emotions picking up their dry cleaning than they do when they're at work. Business doesn't have to be that dry.

No matter how resilient you are, even if you're able to distance yourself from the emotions of others at work, you'd be hard-pressed running away from your own. When you've had a restless night because of stresses in the office, business has become personal. When work gets you down and you grumble and stumble, business has rumbled into your personal life. You know that you haven't been able to escape from this realisation when you feel like a kid unlucky enough to get clothes for Christmas. You might be able to mask your true feelings, but deep down you're seething that Santa could be so insensitive. So impersonal.

It all comes down to this: if there are personnel, it's personal.

Chapter 11

Success is a journey, not a destination

A year ago, I went on a holiday with one of my best friends. Rather than catch a 45-minute plane ride, we thought it'd be a good idea to drive so that we could enjoy the journey. We thought it'd be fun. It wasn't. We thought it'd be easy. It hurt. After driving for five hours, we got lost, only to be told we'd been going round in circles and were really only an hour from where we started. In the middle of summer and in a car with neither air conditioning nor a speedometer, and with only Dr Phil CDs to keep us company, this was the journey from hell. From driving the wrong way onto a one-way bridge to hourly pit stops just to be sick, we were glad to finally arrive at our idyllic beachside retreat 12 hours later, only to be greeted by the worst flooding in a generation, with the roads closed for the weekend. When we finally checked in to our hotel, we didn't care it was so bad there was a sign on the front desk saying 'Room service — straight from our microwave to you!' We were just relieved to have reached our destination. We'd made it. Success, at last. That's one example of why I view the 'Success is a journey, not a destination' cliché with cynicism, because the real joy comes from the destination. And when this cliché is adopted at work, it neglects the five critical elements employees need to be fully engaged and loving their jobs.

Employees need direction

If success is not a destination, then how do you know where you're going? I guess you could retort with the predictable meditative reply, which is to say that you live 'In the now, in this present moment'. While that might be true for some people in their personal lives, at work it's a different story. Most employees need to feel as if they're heading towards something, whatever that something may be. It could be a career goal, an income level, a type of status, or anything that reassures them they're on track to achieve an end goal. Without it, they're just wandering around, wondering what it's all meant to be about. When people climb Mount Everest, they don't do it because they've got nothing else to do on a Sunday morning and so they decide to go for a nice stroll in the Himalayas. They do it because of the thrill, the pride, the curiosity, the marvel of what awaits them when they reach the summit. All of those emotions plus the spectacular views combine to form a unique treasure of immeasurable value they could only achieve by reaching the destination. When people fail to get to the top of Everest, they don't come back down telling their mates, 'Well, at least I got to base camp' or 'At least the journey was lovely'. Without the destination in mind, people wouldn't risk their lives trudging through thick snow and dangerous terrain. Likewise, at work, without a distinct destination in mind, employees won't risk their livelihoods trudging through thick piles of work and mundane terrain.

Employees need support

I don't want to imply the journey is unimportant. It's hugely significant. The destination wouldn't be possible without it. But the problem with this cliché is that it compels people to disregard the destination in favour of the journey, as if one should take precedence over the other. In reality, both need to coexist. Employees don't just require a goal; they require guidance. They don't just desire a career; they desire coaching. They don't just want remuneration; they want resources. All of these fall into the realm of support, which is the role a journey plays in attaining a destination.

When I worked in the corporate world, I wanted to become an operations manager. When the position was finally available, as the leader of the highest-performing team, everyone knew the job was going to be mine — but it wasn't. I didn't get the role. After I finished crying, I went to get some feedback from my manager who, by the way, was more out-of-place in her role than a bikie at a Tupperware party. The only feedback she had for me was that I was 'too much of a people-person', which was apparently a characteristic not suited to this role. So I thought to myself, I'll show her! Resentful and out for vengeful blood, I quickly found a new job with a competing organisation where instead of managing 70 people, I was managing 100. Ha, I've had the last laugh, I thought. Well, no I didn't. My ex-manager was right. I have never ever hated (or bombed) at a job more than this new one. Every second was torture. Every walk down the corridor was like being on death row with the chains of boredom gripped tightly around my wrists and the shackles of disengagement ripping into my ankles and dragging me further and further away from job fulfilment. That wouldn't have happened if my old managers, at any stage during the previous four years, had taken the time to support my destination with a journey of guidance, coaching and resources.

Employees need purpose

In the same way there's no destination without a journey, there is similarly no journey without a destination. This can be seen in the plight of frightened and fleeing refugees who subject themselves to the treacherous journey of a tremendously necessary destination. From sewing their lips shut to going on hunger strikes, and from spending all their money to jeopardising their lives on makeshift boats, this is all part of the journey asylum seekers endure on the way to their destination. The fulfilment of their purpose is of such urgency and significance they'll do anything to get there.

This necessity for purpose also exists at work. Employees need to be able to answer the question 'Why?' to whatever task they're undertaking. Why am I doing this? Why is this important? Why this way? And those answers, when they're clear and strong enough, propel employees to overcome obstacles that would otherwise be insurmountable. When employees work towards an aspiration that's bigger than them, an inspiration with more vigour than them, they'll do almost anything to get there. The challenge comes down to identifying each individual's unique purpose and then finding some way to link it to what they do in their jobs. As the saying goes, it may be that for some employees their whole purpose in life is simply to serve as a warning to others. For the rest, they'll have an untapped talent or a worthy wish that if incorporated into their work, would trash any intransigence.

Employees need internalisation

It's possible I'm yet to change your mind on this cliché. If that's the case, and you still see the journey as being superior to the destination, then at least don't externalise it. Internalisation means that a person's values are congruent with what's happening on their journey, and in a work sense, that employees' values are in sync with the work they're doing. I'm always puzzled by companies when they release values statements, because it's impossible to change an employee's values. You can release a set of company values as a way of guiding your recruitment process, but you can't change what's already ingrained in an employee, often since childhood. Outside of an interview room, there's very little value in values statements. I once had an employee who was a Goth, and so he would answer his phone calls by saying, 'Welcome to XYZ, this is The Devil speaking'. Occasionally he would call himself Death and Dead. There was a total mismatch between his values and the journey he was on at work, so he was dreadfully unsuccessful in his job. He should have worked in a morgue.

Employees need accountability

This cliché is ultimately a cop-out. It's an excuse people use to make failure more palatable. It's a way of consoling someone with the consolation prize of 'Look what you've become through this journey'. If the journey is so much more fantastic than the destination, we'd see people scaling Everest but stopping a metre before the top. 'Ah, that's enough', they'd say. 'I've just come here for the journey.' I've outlined in this book more of my failures than my successes. Granted, that's because I've had more failures than successes. Regardless, there should be no shame in admitting to what you'd hoped for but missed and humbly taking responsibility for it.

Employee ownership is maximised at work not by accepting excuses, but by promoting accountability.

Imagine standing on a never-ending conveyor belt. It's moving but it never ends. Eventually you're going to want to just jump off and say, 'I've arrived'.

Chapter 12

The glass ceiling

It's risky talking about the glass ceiling when you're a bloke. If you're a woman reading this, depending on what I say in the following paragraphs, your opinion of me could be shattered like that ceiling you'd like smashed. But on behalf of other corporate types, I think it's safer for me to talk about this delicate topic because I'm an openly gay man, and often that's worse in the corporate world than being a woman. I reported to an executive for a couple of years who was one of those male chauvinist pigs you want to run over with your car. He was a workplace psychopath and he was noticeably so uncomfortable with my sexuality he would never let me walk behind him. Ever. I'm not sure what he thought I was going to do in the middle of a professional working environment, but nonetheless, he would stand perfectly still with his back against the wall, until I was the one walking in front of him. I confided to a couple of my colleagues — okay, to all of my colleagues — about this strange phenomenon, so we observed him. There were times when I'd be the one to stand perfectly still so he could walk in front of me, but no, it became one of those 'I insist', 'No, I insist', 'No, really, I insist', 'Please, I insist' moments. In the end I would desist. So as you read on, please keep in mind I understand your plight with the glass ceiling despite challenging it as I do.

There was a study conducted by the University of New Mexico that revealed that female managers are more than three times as likely as their male colleagues to underestimate their bosses' opinions of their performance at work. Men, in contrast, were found to *overrate* what their bosses thought of their job performance. These findings subtly suggest maybe it is women who have created the glass ceiling, or at the very least, perhaps they're the ones keeping it going.

I've got a friend who's extremely negative. Unfortunate stuff always seems to happen to her. Yet when I, and others, engage her in conversation, we start to question whether her doom-filled attitude is the consequence of these unlucky incidences or if indeed it's her downbeat predictions that are causing her harm. For example, she'll continuously say things like, 'There aren't any good men in Sydney'. In a city of 4.5 million people, how is that possible? As a result, she's now 29, and over the past decade she's been on fewer dates than a Tibetan monk. She'll say things like, 'All bosses are arseholes'. All of them? So unsurprisingly, she jumps from employer to employer, and sadly, every manager she's had has been incompetent and evil. The most common gripe she'll grumble is, 'I'm getting so old'. She's 29. So of course, she's got about as much energy as a dead snail and every time we talk there's a new injury for us to be updated on. Relating this back to the corporate world, it could be that the person who thinks a glass ceiling exists, the one who subconsciously wants there to be one, is also the person who's most likely to see it. I know many women who refuse to believe in its existence and so their careers keep going from strength to strength.

Mention the term 'office politics' to most people and they'll roll their eyes or scrunch up their face. Tell them it can actually be a good thing and they'll look at you like you're a total disgrace. And yet the higher up you climb the corporate ladder, the more important it is to play the game. As the cartoonist Scott Adams once said, 'Consultants have credibility because they are not dumb enough to work at your company'. Office politics has a bad reputation because of the mudslinging and handwringing that stains it when people don't play fair. But at its core, office politics is just the influencing of others to get what you want. Women seem to be less keen than blokes to play the political game.

I hate office politics. I despise it, but I learnt the importance of learning how to play it when I applied for a promotion once that I didn't get it. The (female) executive's only constructive, but honest, feedback was, 'James, you need to learn that office politics is more important than your experience and qualifications. Here's a book you should read on it so that you've got a better chance next time'. I read the book, and despite it being woeful, I really understood for the first time I needed to master what I'd detested and resisted. Conquering the skill of office politics is more valuable than tapping away at a glass ceiling.

Most women make different choices from their male coun-terparts. For example, studies show women are more likely to give birth than men. I didn't believe this statistic at first, but apparently it's true. Once these children are born, despite there being a rise in the number of men who become stay-at-home dads, it's usually the mothers taking time off work to look after their newborns. And even putting those two aspects aside, men are notoriously more open to the idea of working chronically long hours. It's not that women *can't* do what men do. They can do it all, and better. It's just that women are smart enough to value their life above their work, and so they make decisions to reflect those tendencies.

The impact of this at work can be seen in their capacity to get promoted. If a woman takes a year off for maternity leave, it's difficult to catch up when the business has progressed during the 12 months she was away. It's not impossible; just harder. Thankfully, companies are implementing more and more family-friendly workplaces so this should make it easier for women in the future. But the issue in these instances isn't one of a glass ceiling, but of lifestyle choices. I'm beginning to think it's not so much a glass ceiling. It's a glass labyrinth, as coined by Alice Eagly in her book *Through the Labyrinth*. Navigating to the top of the office hierarchy has less to do with your gender, race, sexuality or any other minority brush you've been painted (or tainted) with, and more to do with how well you're able to steer a course through the amazing maze that is the corporate world.

In Greek mythology, the Minotaur was a beast that had the head of a bull and the body of a man. He was enclosed within an elaborate labyrinth constructed by King Minos on the island of Crete. In a peace deal with King Aegeus, the ruler of Athens, Minos demanded Aegeus send 14 boys and girls to Crete every nine years to be eaten alive by the Minotaur. Aegeus reluctantly agreed. When the time came to send the young children to the labyrinth, Aegeus' son, Prince Theseus, begged his father to be one of the 14. He wanted a chance to kill the Minotaur once and for all. When he arrived in Crete, Minos' daughter, Princess Ariadne, fell in love with Theseus, so she told him how to kill the Minotaur. Ariadne gave Theseus a ball of string and a sword. The ball of string was to be tied to the front door of the labyrinth so that Theseus could easily find his way back, and the sword was to be plunged into the Minotaur's heart. The next morning, Theseus and the other children were shoved into the labyrinth and the door slammed shut behind them. Sticking strictly to the plan, Theseus wound through the complex maze, found the Minotaur, and after a long and tiring battle, the Minotaur was dead.

A similar labyrinth exists in your workplace. Instead of King Minos, you might have King Minus, a boss so worried you'll overtake him he obstructs your progress. Instead of a Minotaur, you might have a dinosaur, a place of work so old school that pagers still adorn the hips of the fellas who swagger from meeting to meeting. Neither of these are permanent blocks. By using a long string of wisdom, or the sharp knife of politicking, you can manoeuvre your way through the corporate maze rather than smashing through an imaginary ceiling, so in the end you get whatever position you desire.

It's true that the number of women in executive positions is miniscule compared to the proportion of women in the workforce, but this is changing. More women are graduating from university. More men are staying home with the kids. More workplaces are becoming family friendly, even as a male executive said to a female friend of mine recently, 'What you see as a glass ceiling, I see as a protective barrier'. Putting aside the attitudes of a small group of small-minded men, the glass ceiling, even if it once existed, has now been glassed. Gail Kelly did it at Westpac. Meg Whitman did it at eBay. Indra Nooyi did it at PepsiCo. Carly Fiorina did it at Hewlett-Packard. In fact, upon becoming the CEO of HP, Carly firmly stated, 'I hope we're at the point that everyone has figured out that there is no glass ceiling'.

Chapter 13

If you build it, they will come

It's very hard to pinpoint the point in history before a cliché is a cliché, when it's planted like a seed in the farmyard of someone's mind, where it sprouts hopeful shoots that fertilise the luscious land of business language. Locating the origin of such clichés is quite difficult. That's not the case with this particular cliché, which comes from a Kevin Costner movie in the 1980s, which says it all, really. Upon hearing an unknown voice in his cornfield telling him 'If you build it, they will come', Costner's character decides to build a baseball field right there in among the corn, setting the scene for a corny cliché that has swept the business world like a torrential downpour drenching a dry landscape. Out of all the clichés in this book, this would have to be the one I *wish* was true. If only business was as easy as building an entity and waiting for them to come. Business failure would be as rare as a Kevin Costner blockbuster.

If this cliché were accurate, there'd be many more successful bloggers in the world. Out of the 110 million blogs that currently exist just a tiny percentage are successful. Whether they're lacking in hits or slacking in comments, most blogs are futile exercises by people desperate for a following. They've usually read a book or attended a seminar or skimmed an article that talked about the power of using a blog to build a profile. So, of course, they set up a blog despite having less to say than a pop-up book, and then blame the blogosphere for not serving up online superstardom. Some bloggers even have the support of mammoth news sites to promote their wares, and even then they're vying for attention like a red-headed stepchild. What they have to say is of such irrelevance, that people don't even care to note their support or disdain by making a simple, effortless comment. Yet, nothing is stopping the tidal wave of millions of new blogs being set up every year, almost all of which are doomed to a short life of irrelevance that no-one besides their loved ones will ever read. And the reason why this occurs is because building it is never enough to make them come.

This cliché neglects the necessity of what is actually being built. The completion of it is one thing, but that isn't enough if people don't want it in the first place. Betamax was a recording cassette-tape released in the '70s that couldn't better-max its main competitor, VHS. As a result, it failed. In the '80s, Coke released a new formula of its famous cola, aptly named New Coke, which left a bad taste in consumers' mouths. It wasn't long before Coke reverted back to its old formula. When Apple spent four years and $50 million developing the Lisa computer, it wasn't to know that another Lisa, this time a Simpson, would characterise its demise. In an episode of *The Simpsons*, Lisa says to

Homer, 'Look at the wonders of the computer age now'. Homer replies, 'Wonders, Lisa? Or blunders?' Lisa retorts, 'I think that was implied by what I said'. Homer sums it up by adding, 'Implied ... or implode?' All three of these products were released by gigantic organisations with huge marketing budgets, extensive research and talented employees, and yet despite these advantages their products weren't embraced by an ordinarily loyal public. Why? Because just building it is never enough to make them come.

Let's assume you do build something magnificent. That alone isn't enough to get people to come unless the marketing is right. In fact, marketing is often more important than the product. I can't think of a single event in the calendar year that excites me more than the Eurovision Song Contest. From the fabulous frocks to the shameless shocks, Eurovision exemplifies the glamour and the glitz, the charm and the cheese that can only be found in Europe. Every year, I hold a Eurovision charity party where like-minded Euro-tragics get together to watch the spectacle on a big screen at the cinema. It usually gets sold out. This year, however, was depressing. Despite getting up to 100 people attending previous events, this year I could only muster 10 of us there. It was like going to a quiet jazz bar and dancing on your own in the centre of a cold and vacant dance floor, and even when the music stops, you keep on dancing slowly to scattered applause. The reason for the poor turnout was marketing. I got lazy. I thought word-of-mouth would be enough, I didn't bother with PR like I had in previous years, and I left the marketing plan to the very last minute. The product was great — it always is. But my marketing let me down. Building it wasn't enough.

This cliché is more incomplete than incorrect. It's missing the bit about marketing and it's dissing the bit about what's being built. It's the E without the mc^2. It's the mousetrap without the rodent snared. It's the tango without two people paired. And that's the problem with a lot of clichés, really. They're so one-dimensional. They sound impressive and at times even inspiring, but in practice they just don't work. Like this one. Just building something won't attract the masses if they think it's about as relevant as a xylophone at an Alice Cooper concert. And they won't come running if they're unaware that the xylophone even exists. The entire formula needs to be in place, and even then nothing is guaranteed.

So let's transfer this cliché to the corporate world where 'If you build it, they will come' works about as well as the Pope starring in *Porky's II*. Just because you hire the right people doesn't mean they'll work well together. Just because you create the best systems doesn't mean people will follow them. Just because you've installed the latest software doesn't mean your staff will adapt. One of my management students implemented a new process within his department and he notified his team of the change via email. After two weeks he noticed his employees had ignored the email and were still using the old procedure. When I asked him how he reacted, his response was, 'Oh, I just sent them another email'. He built the new procedure, yet his team didn't adhere to it. He adopted a communications strategy, yet his team didn't abide by it. What he'd produced had the potential to revolutionise quality and productivity, yet the most vital stakeholders, his employees, simply weren't interested. The mere building of something isn't sufficient for its success, and anyone with an appetite for this cliché really needs to go on a strict diet where the saturated fat of mumbo jumbo is cut out and replaced with a nutritional intake of originality in business language. The excess weight of this cliché's impracticality needs to be shed for the slimmed down rations of logic. It's just junk food for your brain.

Chapter 14

Pick the low-hanging fruit

If the word 'fruit' in this cliché really meant its well-known euphemism for 'gay man', I wouldn't have a problem with it, because then it'd be perfectly reasonable for people to pick the low-hanging fruit. But alas, in the business world, this cliché reflects a persuasion to choose the easy way out. It encourages people to stretch their arms more than they stretch their strengths. It preaches the benefits of what's within reach, but breaches the lessons that the opposite can teach. The low-hanging fruit shouldn't be picked; it should be picketed.

To really get what's wrong with this cliché, you need to understand how orchard workers pick fruit from a tree. They never start at the bottom. They always begin at the top. The pieces of fruit on the highest branches are the ripest since they get more sun than their lower hanging counterparts. This means that the extra time and effort it takes to get to the top is worth it since the quality of the fruit you'll get is superior. People working in the corporate world who crave to start their own business would relate to this. The low-hanging fruit is their job, the regular salary it pays and the security it gives them. The high-hanging fruit is their future business, the windfall it could bring them, and the promise of corporate freedom. Going for the high-hanging fruit can incur an enormous amount of risk and heartache, but if they succeed, it's worth it.

Prior to starting my own business, I was a disengaged employee anxious to get out, but my mind was being polluted by people who were too scared to start a washing machine, let alone a business. It's amusing that those least qualified to give advice are the ones unloading it the most. They'd poison me with low-hanging fruit advice such as, 'But you're doing so well and earning so much' and, of course, the predictable line, 'Don't forget that nine-out-of-10 small businesses fail within two years'. I eventually quit my job and endured years of endless pain and sorrow as I tried to make things work. I sacrificed the second half of my 20s and missed out on a lot of living and loving to land here, but to me, it was worth the struggle. Going for the high-hanging fruit was far more rewarding than staying with the comfort and ease of the low-hanging fruit.

When orchard workers pick the lowest hanging fruit even though they're aware it's inferior to what's located higher up the tree, it shows they're happy forfeiting excellence in favour of a short-term indulgence. Similarly, if you're seen as the type of person who prefers the sloth of low-hanging fruit as opposed to the slog of high-hanging fruit, you're portraying yourself as someone who's indolent and indifferent — not a smart career move. I'm not like that when I'm at work, but I am when I'm at home. For example, cooking is a high-hanging fruit activity. I just don't understand how there could possibly be any enjoyment derived from undertaking a process that takes up to half a day for a consumption period of half a minute. I have a big fridge in my kitchen and in there at the moment are just two items: a carton of milk (which isn't even mine) and a bottle of wine (which most certainly is). So, I refuse to cook. I'm just like Katherine Cebrian when she said, 'I don't even butter my bread; I consider that cooking'. Low-hanging fruit for me is take-away. I buy all of my food ready-to-eat rather than ready-to-make. As a result of my preference for what's quick and easy, I'm forfeiting healthiness (because the nutritional value of take-away is questionable), I'm forfeiting money (because it's cheaper to cook your own meals) and I'm forfeiting fun (since it seems like people take pleasure in cooking for others). I don't deny that it's laziness that's fuelling my behaviour, but at home there's no-one to judge me on this. At work, however, when you focus excessively on low-hanging fruit activities, the interpretation of laziness will still materialise, only the ramifications will be more severe. People will judge you for your disinclination to go for the tougher and riskier activities.

I understand why people at work prefer to pick the low-hanging fruit first. It provides quick wins, scratches nagging items off a lagging to-do list and it's a great PR exercise when the powers-that-be see lots of achievements being made, even though they're negligible in their overall impact. Picking low-hanging fruit is also adopted by those who want to get all the easy stuff out of the way so that it frees them up to focus on more challenging goals. All of it is understandable, but there are a couple of problems with this tactic. Number one, those little tasks might prove to be irrelevant if your high-hanging fruit activities end up taking you in a totally different direction. And number two, when you're finally free to work on those high-hanging aspirations, you might be exhausted. After all the effort you've put into dealing with the low-hanging fruit, by the time you're able to even look at the high-hanging stuff, you find that you've got very little energy left to give. This is another reason why orchard workers start at the top of the tree and work their way down. They carry a bag with them they use to fill with the fruit that they pick. If they were to start at the bottom and work their way up, the bag would just get heavier and heavier as it became full, making their job infinitely more strenuous as they climbed.

There was a time I worked with an executive who was a chronic low-hanging fruit picker. She was three levels above me on the corporate hierarchy, yet it seemed like she was given the wrong position description when she got promoted, because she'd spend all of her time doing our jobs. She'd constantly jump around the office like a jack-in-the-box barking instructions to our employees (when that's what she hired us to do); she'd spend hours graphically designing certificates and banners (when surely her PA could have handled this) and she'd waste her time (and ours) worrying about the most trivial of matters. On one particular occasion, she spent over two and a half hours in a meeting with the entire management team debating whether or not it was appropriate to wear thongs on casual-dress days. I could only sit there flabbergasted, thinking, 'Is she for real?!' Unfortunately, she was as real as the pen I held in my hand that I felt like jabbing into my right eye to divert her attention to more pressing issues. In hindsight, I don't even think that would have worked. We were in effect a leaderless business unit because she exhausted her time and energy dealing with the unimportant low-hanging fruit, leaving her with barely any stamina to tackle the high-hanging fruit, otherwise known as her job.

All this talk of fruit has gotten me hungry. Hungry for managers who dare to let the low-hanging fruit ripen before picking at it with arms that should already be full.

Chapter 15

Hire slow, fire fast

Many managers, burnt by making the wrong decision during the hiring process, vow to always live by this cliché. I understand why. Once you've hired an employee who turns out to be a dud, irreparable damage can be done to the business by the time you're able to fire them. I recall interviewing a gentleman whose entire body was covered in tattoos. But unlike most tattoos which are graphical in nature with dragons, mermaids or their ex-girlfriend's name, this guy's tats were much simpler: what he had tattooed was the trail of his veins. His flesh was marked by ink that traced the outline of his veins all over his legs, his arms, his chest, his neck and even his face. A colleague who joined me for the interview was adamant he shouldn't be hired, but I insisted we give him a shot because it was a non-customer-facing role.

His manner, in stark contrast to his appearance, was lovely, and I feared my colleague was just being discriminatory based on the way he looked.

Within a few months of starting, the trouble began. He would disappear for a week at a time without calling. When he'd turn up for work, he'd hang up on customers whenever they'd ask a tricky question. And he had a habit where he'd rock in his chair non-stop all day long. Back and forth, back and forth, back and forth, so all we'd see was the upper half of his body continuously swinging a metre forward and a metre back, and all we'd hear was the creaking of the chair with every new thrust. Eventually we fired him and it was at that point we were told his veins were tattooed to cover track marks from a drug addiction. I could have used this nasty experience as all the evidence I needed to always hire slow and fire fast, but to discount the merits in doing otherwise never made sense.

Slowing the hiring process doesn't guarantee the quality of your decisions. If your recruitment process is ineffective, it doesn't matter how long it takes to decide who you'll hire, the negative outcome will still be the same. If you've got friends who keep choosing the wrong partner, you'll see this factor play out prominently in their lives. When a woman keeps choosing to date blokes who are bad for her, it has little relevance whether it takes her a day to decide who she'll be with or a year. Of greater significance is the decision-making process she's using to figure out who she'll start seeing. If that's flawed, then the duration of the process isn't important because the outcome will still be the same.

Similarly, what influences the quality of your new hires isn't how fast or slow it takes you to make a decision, but rather the robustness of the process you're using. With any other process in the workplace, managers would never tell their staff to slow it down or make it longer. Imagine a sign in a bank, 'Dear Customers, it's our pleasure to announce the length of our queues have now increased from a wait time of 15 minutes to the new period of two hours. We hope you enjoy this latest process improvement, so please take a number and get comfortable. We'll be with you as late as possible. Have a nice day. Management'.

Taking your time with the hiring process might work when you're trying to snap up mediocre employees with nowhere to go, but the most talented people who are high in demand are unlikely to wait around. The longer you wait to make a decision, the higher the likelihood of your competitors recruiting them instead. For the sake of using another cliché, it really is 'first in, best dressed'. Bargain shoppers understand this concept well. I experience a mixture of amusement and astonishment every year when I see images of the Boxing Day sales on TV where hundreds of people gather outside department stores just before opening time so they can literally be the first in, best dressed. As the doors open at 9 am, in their eagerness to snatch up a good deal, these shoppers will run and push and trample and elbow and dive, almost as if they're in an action-packed adventure film. The only difference is instead of saving a pretty girl from an evil warlord, they're saving a penny on a matching bathrobe and shower cap. Even so, they totally get that a good deal won't hang around forever, just like the most talented employees.

There's a clear purpose for recruiting a new employee: to fill a gap in the business. For as long as that gap remains unfilled, it's costing you money. So, yes, hire slow if you must, but keep in mind the opportunities being wasted as a result of the unnecessary delay. I had a manager who would prolong the recruitment process for no other reason than to save money. In her mind, the longer she took to fill a role, the fewer wages she had to pay in the short term. So while she was happy her bottom line hadn't bottomed out, the rest of us were burdened with a bigger workload. We became more frantic than the hyped-up hosts of late-night tele-shopping commercials. What we longed for was the work atmosphere of the seductive 'Call me, call me now' ads. Instead, we resembled the frenzied 'But wait, there's more' variety. And since we were understaffed, there was always more that needed to be done, which limited our capacity to take advantage of money-making opportunities that came our way. Our manager's short-sightedness had her focused only on the immediate benefit of salary savings, and not on the negative impact of opportunity cost. In the end, everyone lost.

The other half of this cliché's equation is the 'fire fast' reference. There are certain situations where this is warranted, such as with criminal offences and gross incompetence. The group one level up from these people is best described by George Carlin: 'Most people work just hard enough not to get fired and get paid just enough money not to quit'. But sometimes managers rush to the termination option before they've had a crack at other avenues of increasing performance, such as motivation and development. It might take more effort in the short term, but it tends to pay off in the long term. A lot of managers don't realise some of the most loyal workers they'll ever have are those they took the time and care to develop, especially if the rate of transformation has been significant.

Out of all the possible combinations of this cliché, which one is the most appropriate? Hire fast, fire fast? Hire fast, fire slow? Hire slow, fire fast? Hire slow, fire slow? The answer will depend on the complexities of the role, the character of the employee, your contribution to their success or failure and so many other factors that it's irrational to blindly accept just one of these combinations without considering each unique situation. To adopt just one of these and ignore the others would be to fail fast and grow slow.

Chapter 16

What gets measured gets done

Left-brain thinkers have taken over the working world. Instead of hearts and souls, we get charts and goals. Many executives make the transition from careers as accountants and economists into the realm of leading people and assume numbers and stats will motivate. Like a jilted ex-lover, they bring with them the baggage of quantifiable data, the emotional scars of debits and debtors and the sentimental ballads of balance sheets. All of this serves its purpose in a financial sense, but it's nonsensical to think employees will achieve what you desire just because you're able to apply a calculator to every aspect of their performance. This cliché results in arduous amounts of time tediously preparing performance appraisals, which in themselves are poor-performing. In fact, if performance appraisals were put through a performance appraisal they would get a 'does not meet expectations'. They're a waste of time and money, and why companies continue to persevere with this outdated performance management process that is despised as much by managers as it is by employees is beyond comprehension.

The problem with managers who subscribe to the ludicrous cliché of 'What gets measured gets done' is they start to measure everything. They get carried away like a Hollywood star in a medicine cabinet, and before they know it, employees are overwhelmed. They get bombarded with so many targets to focus on they end up losing track of what's important and what's not. With their attention scattered and their gumption shattered, their performance levels drop. So an additional measure that was initiated as a way of increasing productivity ends up decreasing it because of an overzealous management mentality that looks for an easy way out of motivating people intrinsically.

If what gets measured really does get done, then surely we'd see evidence of it working in the public arena. Despite there being 36 signatory countries to the Kyoto Protocol, at the time of writing, only a few countries are on track to meet their emissions targets. Despite Bob Hawke's quantifiable promise in 1987 that no Australian child will be living in poverty by 1990, there are still over 500 000 Aussie kids living in poverty today. And despite a whole range of data showing a greater impact on healthcare and violence caused by alcohol and cigarettes, the world still spends trillions of dollars pursuing a war on drugs. Put simply, setting a measure is not in itself enough to achieve that measure. Sure, it can be a helpful start and a handy benchmark, but unless it's followed through with intention and commitment, it's destined for the dustbin. To paraphrase Peter De Vries, it's like wanting to be a writer when you can't stand paperwork. It's the same reason why I found *The Secret* (both the book and the DVD) such an incomplete piece of work. The overriding message is that if you set a specific goal and do all the prescribed affirmations and positive thinking, eventually you'll attract into your life whatever it is you want. Yet, I can repeat an affirmation a million times that the charcoal-coloured chair I'm sitting on will turn into a crimson red, but unless I get up and paint it, it's never going to be red — no matter how positively I think about it.

In their hurried attempts to measure all that can be measured, panicky managers end up measuring the wrong things. As an example, let's take the most unnecessarily overly measured department in any organisation: the call centre. Managers of these already high-pressured environments measure everything from the number of calls per hour, to the length of each call; from the time they show up, to the speed they follow-up; from the words they use, to the sales they make. Instead, they should be a little more considerate of their employees since they already put up with an endless stream of whinging customers. I know of one very large financial services call centre that measures the length of their employees' *toilet breaks*. Imagine sitting on the loo and trying to hurry a process that needs to be eased, not squeezed. It gives a whole new meaning to the term 'Managing the bottom line', that's for sure.

No matter how hard people try, there are some things that simply can't be measured — and yet they critically need to be accomplished within every workplace. Take trust, for instance. How do you measure the level of trust employees have for their manager? You can't. And yet without trust, you can forget about getting any traction with engagement, performance and loyalty. How do you measure creativity? I guess you could look at the number of ideas generated, but that's more innovation than creativity. Creativity is the uniqueness that we bring to an established task while innovation is the introduction of a new initiative. It would be virtually impossible to quantify creativity.

And then there are personalities. How do you measure someone's personality? Yes, there are profiling systems, such as Myers-Briggs, which are mind-boggling in their accuracy, but they are not measurements. My point is this: if you pursue the theory of 'What gets measured gets done', this will likely result in the neglect of the far more significant aspects of the workplace that can't be measured. You can add to that list other immeasurable necessities like relationships, passion and hope, to really understand Albert Einstein when he said, 'Not everything that can be counted counts, and not everything that counts can be counted'. Then again, you might totally disagree, and think all of these factors are irrelevant. With your alpha-male machismo, you presume passion is for pansies and trust is the financial fund you've set up for your kids. Or perhaps in your shoulder-padded corporate suit, you think relationships are merely a rung to be used to help you smash the glass ceiling, and Hope is the name of your first-born child you haven't seen awake since returning to work. If you fall into either of those two categories, I wish you well — and karma.

So really, this is all about smacking. An abundance of measures are a micromanager's way of smacking a subordinate into action. They're there as a punishment rather than a reward. It's like being in a fetish dungeon where the dominatrix is the manager, the slave is the employee and the weapons are these strangling measures. It's a form of negative motivation, which in itself is an oxymoron. If negative motivation worked, we wouldn't have an increasing rate of recidivism within our prison system and our jails wouldn't be overcrowded. If negative motivation worked, kids with overbearing and controlling parents wouldn't grow up to become insecure and shy people, unable to think for themselves or make their own decisions. If negative motivation worked, dictators of nations would respond to crippling and punitive sanctions, instead of hardening their resolve and resorting to terrorism.

A perfect example of this negative motivation can be seen in Roald Dahl's remarkable book, *Matilda*. In one scene, the sinister school principal, Agatha Trunchbull, screeches, 'My school is a model of discipline! Use the rod, beat the child, that's my motto. They're all mistakes, children! Filthy, nasty things. Glad I never was one'. She later adds, 'I have never been able to understand why small children are so disgusting. They're the bane of my life. They're like insects: they should be got rid of as early as possible. My idea of a perfect school is one in which there are no children … at all'. Do you have a bit of Trunchbull in your management style?

As the German proverb goes, the main thing is to keep the main thing the main thing. To do otherwise is to fall into the trap of what gets measured gets done, or rather, what gets measured gets undone. You'll find when you choose the three most vital goals to measure, achieving those will have a flow-on effect to all the other KPIs you care about. There's no need to barrage and berate, belittle and backdate.

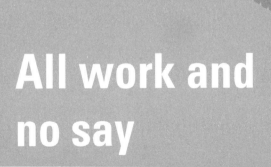

Part IV

All work and no say

Chapter 17

If it ain't broke, don't fix it

I must admit I'm not really a Meatloaf fan. It's just not my kind of music. I have a simple rule when it comes to the music I tune in to: if there aren't back-up dancers or costume changes, I'm not interested. But there is one particular Meatloaf song I adore, if not for its screaming lyrics and cranking crescendo, then certainly for its message. The track, titled 'If it ain't broke, break it', is all about being counterintuitive, especially when faced with adversity. And it really does make sense. Those who broker the cliché of, 'If it ain't broke, don't fix it', prefer the monotonous saneness of sameness.

My dad has said to me on more than one occasion, 'Son, if I'm not perfect, what chance has anybody else got?' He was joking. (I think). Anyway, I get his point. No-one and nothing is perfect, which means there's always room for improvement. If we need to wait until something is broken before fixing it, we're ignoring the fact that everything can be enhanced. There was nothing really the matter with horses and buggies, typewriters and candles. But cars, laptops and light bulbs were a welcome fix. There's a certain arrogance that appears in people who assume the status quo is perfectly fine. Perhaps they're afraid of change. Maybe they're afraid of chance. Whatever it is, they hold themselves back by assuming they only need to act when stuff goes wrong, which all along just prolongs the inevitable.

Something doesn't need to be broken in order for it to be repaired. Take a table, for instance. A table can be perfectly operational yet still need repairing. It might be a scratch that needs smoothing or a leg imbalance that needs levelling, but whatever it is, the table is still functional. It ain't broke, but by fixing it up, it ups its level of effectiveness. The same reasoning applies to every aspect of your workplace: from processes in your team to their level of esteem; from your personnel rules to your training room tools; from your computer-based systems to your enragement-based symptoms. All of it can be fixed... even if it ain't broke. Waiting until something is broken before becoming a Mr or Ms Fix-it is like not bothering to brush your teeth because, hey, they still work and they're still in your mouth. Eventually the problem will just come back to bite you.

The world is advancing at a faster pace than at any point in history. If you're thinking, 'Thank you, Captain Obvious', no doubt you've already heard that statement from people trying to convince you to cherish change. But here's something a little extra. When people consider the pace of change, they think about it linearly, when in fact the accelerating speed of change, particularly in regards to technology, is not linear. It's exponential. It gets faster and faster. This means that when gurus say we'll have a certain capability in 20 years' time, they're just basing that figure on today's rate of progress. What it actually means is it's likely to come true in *five* years' time when you factor in that next year's technological change will be more rapid than this year's, and the following year's more rapid than the one that preceded it, and so on. So the danger for those who follow the 'If it ain't broke, don't fix it' line is they'll be left trying to catch up to the rest of us who have moved on. Instead of it being a world of leaders and followers, it'll be a world of leaders, followers and wallowers. The wallowers will be the stubborn folk whose hero is the tortoise that won the race against the hare in Aesop's famous fable. 'Slow and steady wins the race' is the motto they'll mutter while conveniently ignoring the hare only lost by a hair's-breadth even though it took a nap. The wallowers will be left behind like a fart in the breeze, hanging around long enough and strong enough to continue to be of discomfort to others who have dared to choose progress over stagnation.

This cliché also implies you shouldn't take risks. After all, there's a level of risk involved when you try to fix something that isn't broken. But what exactly are you risking? The wonderful thing about the status quo is that you can return to it at any time. Whenever you get that sentimental urge, just stay perfectly still, and in a split second you'll be back there, reunited with your long-lost love of the stale and ordinary. You're free to choose whether you'd like to be a Flintstone or a Jetson. But while the rest of us are travelling freely through space in flying aircrafts, your alternative will be to get around in a prehistoric car made of stone, powering it with your bare feet and instead of yabba-dabba-doo'ing, you'll be yabba-dabba-going backwards. The bigger question is which of the two options poses the greater risk. I like to be guided by Brian Tracy, who said that the greatest risk of all is to not take risks. And keep in mind the difference between 'taking a risk' and 'being risky'. The former means to make a calculated assessment before taking a chance, while the latter is to be reckless and overconfident in your behaviour.

Sometimes you don't even realise something is broken until you try fixing it, which is why I get so perplexed with exit interviews. They're too little too late. It's just like being married to someone who asks you for a divorce, but then you wait until after the divorce has been finalised, the house is sold and shared child custody starts, before you finally ask your ex-spouse, 'So, do you mind telling me why you wanted to break up?' But if prior to the exit interview, and prior to the resignation and prior to disengagement setting in, we attempted to fix something that didn't appear to be broken, then it's unlikely we would have gotten to the exit interview stage so soon.

Before a bird is born, an egg must first be hatched. Initially a few cracks begin to appear, and then it breaks open as the newborn flaps its wings and wanders into the world. Unless the egg is broken, that beautiful and bony baby bird would never even have the chance to fly, let alone soar. It always begins with something being broken.

Chapter 18

Work smarter, not harder

Since when did work get such a bad name? Too many people despise what they spend most of their life doing. Referring to their work despairingly as 'just a job', they resign before they've resigned. They spend their time searching for short cuts, all the while undercutting their own personal growth and progress. To them, work is something to be avoided, not something to be enjoyed and applauded. The result is a philosophy to stop working hard. They vow to work smart, whatever that means. It sounds good, anyway. The way they denounce hard work, you'd think they were working on tractors rather than business plans; lifting slabs of concrete rather than pens and paper, and climbing the pyramids rather than the corporate ladder. Most people working in an office wouldn't know hard work if it hit them on the head with a hole puncher.

Roger Federer is considered to be the greatest tennis player of all time. Would you say he works hard? The hours he spends each day rigorously practising his craft, the pain and sweat of his gruelling training schedule and the sacrifices he's made in order to become the best, all suggest that yes, he works pretty hard. Hillary Clinton is deemed by millions to have one of the sharpest minds in politics. Would you say she works hard? The exhausting schedule she subjects herself to during election campaigns, the mercilessness of a salivating media monitoring her every move and the careful tact and diplomacy she needs to attach to every word she utters, all suggest that yes, she also works pretty hard. Smarts are certainly involved, but in both of these cases, neither Roger nor Hillary would have achieved their success and international standing if it weren't for a lot of hard work. So to ignore what Thomas Jefferson once said, 'I'm a great believer in luck and I find the harder I work, the more I have of it', is to disregard that hard work is an imperative component of exceptional success. Alas, more people seem to be inspired by Edgar Bergen's famous quote, 'Hard work never killed anybody, but why take a chance?'

The 'work smarter, not harder' cliché instructs its followers to substitute hard work for smart work. But you can't work smarter *instead of* harder. They can't be swapped flippantly like gossip in a trailer park hair salon. Smart work is the subsequence of hard work. You can only work smarter once you've slogged it out in the zone of hard work; once you've sweated and sworn, been beaten and torn, by the rough and tumble of experience. Because only then will you know what it takes to really work smarter. I don't begrudge smart work. But I do prejudge those who think they can avoid hard work in pursuance of glory.

In this day and age where people are more highly educated than at any point in history, chances are your competitors are as smart, if not smarter, than you. To outsmart them would be a tough strategy. But to 'out-hard work' them is a wiser choice. People might have the brains, but most don't have the grunt. What they have in intellect, they often lack in determination, doggedness and drive. Think of this as your diamond scheme, since the diamond is the hardest natural substance on Earth. Your aim is to be the hardest; not the smartest. Outlast them, don't outclass them. It amazes me how swiftly people give up. From new businesses to new diets, so many well-meaning souls abandon their plans for reasons not to do with intelligence, but with tenacity.

I wouldn't mind the 'work smarter, not harder' chestnut so much if the word 'not' was replaced with the word 'and' so that it became 'work smarter *and* harder'. The two can coexist. While one blows the metaphorical trombone of smartness, the other flows with the metaphysical grindstone of hard work. It's a big risk to separate working smarter from working harder. It's much wiser to make the most of both.

Working harder doesn't need to involve working longer hours. Working harder merely means that we make the mental capacity available to accommodate it in our lives. It's about what we're doing during the hours we've worked rather than the duration of time that we're laboriously labouring. The two main areas that hamper hard work are procrastination and distractions. I used to suffer from a severe problem of procrastination. In 2006 I spent more time procrastinating than working. I'd spend half a day staring at a blank screen, thinking if I just looked hard enough maybe the work would take care of itself. I'd take days to complete a task that should have only taken an hour. I'd run away from the agonising thought of work like an unfaithful husband outrunning his wife's shotgun. And then there were distractions. During that period I was more distracted than a redneck at a family reunion — and nowhere near as busy as one. I would relish every opportunity to have my attention diverted, getting strayed by Facebook, being transfixed by the trance of TV, browsing the net, sleeping in, calling a friend, consulting the fridge and all the while digging a ditch that got deeper and deeper and deeper. Collectively, I wasted weeks and weeks by being weak-willed and unfocused. My ability to earn money was squandered. Unfed and fed up, in January 2007 I made that year 'The Year of No Procrastination and Distractions'. It worked. I turned the habit of laziness into the habit of hard work by making the unwavering decision to do so.

When many people say they put in 110 per cent at work, I think they mean over the space of a week. Hard work doesn't need to be such a bad thing.

Chapter 19

Let's give it 110 per cent

This cliché is a favourite among managers who aspire to be motivational speakers. Unable to come up with more creatively enticing phraseology to push their troops into action, they resort to the idiot idiom of 'Let's give it 110 per cent'. I had a manager who used this as the solution to every problem. Productivity is down? Let's give it 110 per cent. Sales are falling? Let's give it 110 per cent. Run out of useful things to say? Let's give it 110 per cent. I would observe him in meetings because I was fascinated by the many different ways he was able to use this cliché. Sometimes he'd demand it: 'I want to see 110 per cent effort as of yesterday!' when he was unlikely to get much out of us today let alone the day before. At other times he'd be encouraging: 'If we give this 110 per cent, I think we'll see results' when the only results he could get us interested in were the office sweepstakes. But no matter what tone he used to communicate this useless formation of words, we would walk away from his office feeling less inspired than when we walked in.

The trouble with the exertion of 110 per cent effort is it's a mathematical impossibility. If you know of any managers saying this cliché who happen to work in accounts or finance, it's probably a good idea to check their credentials. They might have bought their degree off the internet in a package deal consisting of diet pills and a Russian girl named Olga. The reality is we only have 100 per cent of ourselves to give. I can't get 110 per cent juice out of an orange, but I can try to get 100 per cent of its juice into a glass. I can't get 110 per cent out of a book, but I can make myself read 100 per cent of the text. I can't get 110 per cent out of a car, but I can press on the accelerator to reach 100 per cent of its speed. Our maximum output is precisely that: our maximum. Anything extra requires a miracle … or good drugs.

If you tried to run a motor at 110 per cent, there's only one thing that would happen: it would get burnt out. It would splutter and cough, rumble and convulse, then give up. A similar thing happens with humans. It's the reason why people have nervous breakdowns, or go on stress leave, or suffer from preventable injuries. Their mental and physical capabilities have been reached and upon being forced to go further than is possible, their bodies vehemently react in a way that lets them know it's not going to happen.

I used to work with a young lady who had a three-level warning system that would let us know she was close to reaching her pressure limit. We knew she'd arrived at level one when we'd hear her scraping the ground of her Zen garden. The scrape, scrape, scrape of the miniature shovel against the sand would put us on high alert. We knew she'd arrived at the more hot-tempered level two when we'd hear her stress marbles bumping into each other in the palm of her hand. The click, clack, clang of the two spheres would shorten our breath cycle and increase our heart rate as we waited to see if she'd explode. And then we knew she'd reached the threshold of her intensity when we'd hear the almost-violent tapping of her knuckles against the fishbowl on her desk while water splashed all over her in-tray. It's no surprise the fish eventually died. It was a surprise, however, when she emailed the entire organisation to let everyone know the fish had died and the funeral would be held in the women's toilets on Friday at 11 am. The fish carked it on a Tuesday. I think she wanted to give people time to prepare, or at the very least, find something to wear. This raises two pertinent questions: where did she keep the dead animal during this time and what possessed five people to attend the funeral in a women's-only toilet cubicle? Nonetheless, she was a lady who was acutely aware of her emotional and physical limitations. Trying to push her beyond those limits risked that she would quit, and in the end, she did. Her 100 per cent effort might not have been as much as someone else's 100 per cent effort, but it was still the maximum capability and capacity she had.

It's baffling that managers think they would be able to get 110 per cent out of their staff when most, if not all, employees would struggle putting in even 100 per cent. Imagine how exhausting it would be if you always worked at full throttle. I don't think it's possible. Your best performers probably fluctuate throughout the day within the 80 to 95 per cent range; your B-grade workers will fluctuate within the 60 to 80 per cent category; and then you'll have the rest floating somewhere along the zero to 60 per cent scale. No matter where your mental and physical exertion lies throughout the day, it's unlikely any of that variance is influenced by your boss telling you to put in 110 per cent. I've had jobs where I've put in maximum effort. I'd work 14 hours a day, seven days a week, with full concentration and dedication. At no time did it feel like I was pushing myself too hard. I did it because I felt the job was important and pleasurable, which are two vital components in getting employees to be proactive. But then there were other jobs where I'd surf the internet more than the intranet, send personal emails more than business emails and I knew exactly which keyboard button to press so that whenever my boss walked past, a spreadsheet would replace the *Better Homes and Gardens* website. Yet it was in the latter job where my manager would egg us on to deliver 110 per cent. Did it work? No. Why? Well, empty rhetoric is just that. Empty.

Employees use the 110 per cent cliché as often as managers. When they're trying to impress their superiors, they vow to put in 110 per cent to meet a certain target with a 'you can count on me' aura of bravura. Obviously an exaggeration, this claim can be trusted about as much as a Nigerian widow telling you via email she'll give you half of her husband's $20 million estate if you just hand over your bank details. I tend to raise my eyebrow at these 110 per cent promises and reply with, 'Oh? And just how do you propose to do that?' They can do their best, yes. But to put in more than is humanly possible is implausible.

I totally understand managers don't literally expect 110 per cent from their employees. What they're implying is that what they desire is more than the ordinary output. Fine. Then let's just say that. There's no need for redundant terms like 110 per cent. It's just like the incoherent term, 'you know'. I had a manager who was a chronic you-knower. 'You know, the fact is that our productivity is, you know, less than, you know, it was this time last year, and you know, if that doesn't change, you know, your KPIs won't be achieved, you know what I mean?' In meetings, I would keep a tally of her ramblings to pass the time. In one meeting alone, she mentioned 'you know' 64 times. The 110 per cent statement is just as irrelevant. Know what I mean?

Chapter 20

Work/life balance

When I was a young child, my parents refused to let my sisters and me believe in Santa Claus. Remaining ever conscious about the feelings of other kids, they would repeatedly warn us not to ruin the yuletide spirit for our friends, so we were forbidden from uttering a word about the truth while we were at school. As 25 December approached, our friends would be getting revved up about Rudolph, excited about the elves and prattling on about presents underneath the Christmas tree, while my sisters and I would remain obediently quiet as we sat back and just thought, 'Suckers'.

And so it is with work/life balance. Millions of people have been sucked into believing this thing that doesn't exist. They relentlessly chase the ever-elusive goal like a kid yearning to get onto Santa's list of who's naughty and nice. They look at when they're working, they don't dare to stay back late and they know if they've been bad or good, so they're good for goodness sake — all for the fiction of a work/life balance.

What's absurd about this cliché is the implication work and life are opposites. The insinuation seems to be that the two terms are territorial enemies terrorising its owner for attention. But they're not warring opposites at all. They coexist together within the same life. People think fire and water are opposites, but they're just two elements coexisting on the same planet. People think Israel and Palestine are opposites, but they're just two groups trying to coexist in the same region. People think that Mrs Mangel and Madge were opposites, but they were just two residents trying to coexist on the same street.

It's when you deem two sides to be opposites that trouble starts to brew. Here's what I mean. Those who get turned on by fire and water as enemies will set something alight for the sake of putting it out. Those who see Israel and Palestine as enemies will try to defeat the other at any cost. And when Mrs Mangel and Madge saw one another as enemies, they would sting each other with nasty words and feisty put-downs like, 'You're ruining my life, you vixen!' when one of them spilled nail polish on a doily. Likewise, when you interpret work and life as being two sides of a coin, conflict is inevitable. The first step in taking control of both your work and your life is to stop seeing one as the flipside of the other. They can both coexist.

I'm a Libran. If you were to check out my astrological charts, they'd tell you people with my star sign long for desirability (tick — growing up, I wanted to be more famous than Cher), are bossy (tick — at school I'd finger-point more than I'd finger-paint), are slight perfectionists (tick — that should bee obvious too yew bye now) and since we're represented by scales, we're supposedly balanced (not sure about that one). I can't recall a single time I've had a work/life balance. There've been periods where I've worked like a machine and others where I've worked like a frog, where my work ethic has been more jumpy and slippery than anything else. But I've never had a real balance between the two. Looking back, I now know the way we spend our hours will never be in balance. They'll vary from day to day. This week it might skew towards work and next week it might tilt towards life. It might be one way when you're younger and totally different when you're older. It could lean towards work when you're single and life when you're married — or vice versa. The point I'm making is work/life balance is not about doing things in proportion. It's about doing what feels right … right now. If you imagine your time as being represented by Libran scales, where work is on one side and life is on the other, they'll rarely ever be balanced. Every now and again the scales will tip to one side and then to the other and back again and back again and back again …

Ron White once quipped, 'People are saying that I'm an alcoholic, and that's not true, because I only drink when I work, and I'm a workaholic'. A colleague of mine works more hours than a 7-Eleven, and if he drank on the job, Foster's would put a brewery on his front lawn. He sleeps for only three hours a night (at best) and works during every other minute seven days a week, and despite earning over $1 million a year, he hasn't been on a holiday in two decades and has no intention of ever going on one. That sounds far-fetched, I know, but I promise it's true. Yet if you were to ask him if he's got a work/life balance, he'd respond with an emphatic 'yes', because in his mind, work and life shouldn't be separate. He feels balanced. Work is life and life is work. To me, his routine is as torturous as listening to karaoke, but it shows that there isn't a perfect work/life tune that suits all people. The ideal work/life rhythm for one individual is like a melody of nails being scraped down a blackboard for another. With differing needs, priorities and preferences, the work/life balance imposition on one and all is impractical.

So if work/life balance is obsolete, there has to be an alternative. One option is *work/life integration*. This is where work and life get married. You recognise they don't have to be compartmentalised, so there's no need to aspire for an equal balance between the two. Instead, a more fluid approach is adopted where you effortlessly weave in and out from one to the other. Work doesn't have to be an anti-life experience. By integrating work and life, your work friends become life friends, and your life passions enter your work practices. I agree with Mickey Rooney when he said, 'Always get married early in the morning. That way, if it doesn't work out, you haven't wasted a whole day'. His point? At least give it a go. From the outside, work/life integration can seem disintegrative, but on the inside, there are few moments as fulfilling as the congruence between work and life.

The second option is *work/life choices*. This is when work and life get divorced. If you decide your career is what drives you more than anything else, then don't feel guilty about not having enough 'me time'. And if you decide you want your time on earth to be about 'life', then that's fine, too, but then don't complain about a limited career. With work/life choices, you sacrifice one for the other only if you're happy doing so. I was at a networking event where I struck up a conversation with a couple who were on their first date. Odd place for a date, I thought, but then again, they were odd. The man had been married and divorced four times while the woman had been married and divorced three times. I incredulously asked the guy if all of this puts him off getting married again. His response was, 'No, I'm really looking forward to my next divorce'. Likewise, look forward to divorcing yourself from either work or life so long as the option you're left with is aligned, not maligned, with your values — the person you really are.

Chapter 21

Failure is not an option

When we teach children the multiplication tables, we'd never dream of warning them 'failure is not an option'. If they're learning to ride a bike and happen to fall off, we don't curl our lips and lecture them on the unacceptability of failure. If they're learning the alphabet and they keep getting stuck at the letter F, we don't roar with a fierce, 'Do you know what the letter F stands for? Failure! What have I told you about failure?' We don't do any of that. Responsible parents are calm and patient with their children. They know for a fact failure *is* an option, and so they find ways to help their kids overcome it. But with adults, we're not so generous — especially in work situations. When projects are started, employees are told failure is not an option. When pitches for new accounts occur, sales reps are told failure is not an option. And when, in our eyes, people at work have failed us, we take mental notes for future reference. Or as was the case with one guy I worked with, he'd take 'revenge notes' where he'd list potential acts of retribution next to the names of those who'd hurt him. It wouldn't have been so alarming had he not looked like a serial killer.

The first thing this cliché creates is atychiphobia — a fear of failure. Employees become too afraid to take risks. They worry about being punished. When errors occur, they cover them up to avoid being reprimanded. They fret over what could go wrong rather than what might go right. They withdraw, since that's a safer option. A similar thing happens to people in their personal lives. Take me, for instance. I have a fear of failure when it comes to approaching people who I like in a bar or a club. I'll stare from a distance but I'll never go up and say hi. The fear of being rejected and looking foolish is far too great. The result? My definition of a long-term relationship is four months. The fear of failure can be crippling and it stems from the 'failure is not an option' cliché. At work, ironically, by instilling in people a fear of failure in the hope they'll succeed, that very fear becomes an impediment to the success desired. And all of this happens because employees are smart enough to know that failure is always an option, irrespective of how unattractive that scenario may be to an employer.

Stating 'failure is not an option' is too vague because it all depends on your definition of the word 'failure'. Would you say Jesus was a failure? Whether or not you're a Christian, it's an interesting question to ponder. Using the conventional interpretation, Jesus would definitely be a failure because in the end he was crucified. But when you take into account he's the source of hope and goodwill for billions of people, it's difficult to consider him as being anything other than a stellar success. How about an Olympic athlete who only manages to place fourth in a race? By traditional standards, that person could also be thought of as a failure since she would have gone home without a medal. But when you take into account that she only lost by a couple of seconds and is by far the fastest in her country, it's unfair to brand her as anything other than an inspirational winner. The fuzzy meaning of the word 'failure' renders this cliché about as useful as a pedal-powered wheelchair. You want your employees to get moving, but the tool you've provided leaves them powerless, or to twist the well-known expression, up shit creek without a pedal.

Failure should always be an option. To avoid talking about it is to be like those people who look as if they're upset but when you ask them what's wrong, they respond with a sulky, 'Nothing'. Knowing they're feeling down, you press further: 'I can tell something's the matter. What's up?' And yet, despite looking like they've just repeatedly watched the scene from *Beaches* where what's-her-face dies, they still respond with a whimper of, 'Nothing'. This process continues until the consoler either gives up trying to be the wind beneath their wings, or actually gives them something to be miserable about. The best managers don't work in that denial space. They plan for the worst-case scenario so that they're prepared should it occur. To say failure is not an option cuts you and your team off from the possibility it might happen, leaving you in a potentially precarious predicament.

If you work in emergency services and lives are at stake, I guess it's understandable for failure to never be an option. But for other types of work, failure is a necessary constituent of innovation, creativity, personal growth and performance mastery. In my late teens I was a turndown attendant for one of Sydney's most glamorous hotels. I was a housekeeper who'd go from room to room every night making the beds, cleaning the toilets and placing a chocolate on each pillow.

My supervisor would examine the rooms afterwards to see if I was doing a good job. She'd put on a clean glove and swipe her long finger along the appliances to test for dust. She'd check the beds to make sure I'd made them tight enough so a tucked-in guest would be stuck in there. And she'd inspect the shower doors so there wasn't a hint of lint left over from the towels. This was a job where I was continuously failing. From leaving dirty rags on bathroom floors to rummaging through chests of drawers, from eating leftover food off room-service trays to helping myself to guests' eau de toilettes, I was a professional failure. Despite this being an establishment where the highest standards needed to be upheld, I was always allowed to fail. It was never frowned upon. It was never forbidden. It was never punished. When one of the world's finest hotels sees the benefits of letting staff fail, anyone can.

Ronald Reagan notably advised, 'You can tell a lot about a fellow's character by the way he eats jelly beans'. While that may be true, you can also tell a lot about people by the way they respond to failure. Sometimes it's more essential for people to recover from failure than to experience success. The way they react when circumstances don't go their way is an invaluable way of identifying their true nature. To remove failure as an option is to be without this test of their temperament when they're bombarded with pressure or disappointment.

To say failure is not an option is in itself an utter failure.

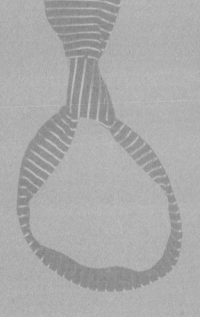

Part V

Paying flip service

Chapter 22

The customer is always right

Some people were born to work in customer service. No matter how vicious and vile a customer becomes, these smiling starlets still sympathise and pamper them because, yes, the customer is always right, and yes, without customers we wouldn't have a business and yes, it's important to exceed customers' expectations. Whatever. I've always struggled with blindly assuming the customer is always right. In fact, on so many occasions I would make it my mission to prove them wrong. Maybe that's why I became a consultant.

I attended a customer service course ... once. Never again. Half a day was painfully spent on 'What is a customer?' I found it unusual no-one replied with 'a pain in the arse', which is what many of them can be. But not mine. My customers are marvellous. Perhaps I'm just fortunate enough to have the luxury of choosing who I work with, or maybe I'm just plain lucky. Regardless, no manager can say with a straight face the customer is always right when so many of them are bothersome and blatantly incorrect. Your employees will never take you seriously when you dribble such drivel. Sometimes customers need to be educated.

Managers who subscribe to one management cliché usually subscribe to most of them — even when they're contradictory. For example, managers who claim the customer is always right imply that customers are above employees on the hierarchy of stakeholders. But at the same time, these same managers will assert employees are their greatest asset. Well, which is it? Because it's important to make a decision — and it can't be both. If it's the customer you prize the most, then that's bound to have a demoralising effect on your employees, and if your employees are feeling downtrodden, your customers will be trotted upon with the hooves of bad moods and the legs of intolerance. If you're after customer service that's delightful, then you need to treat your employees delightfully. Acknowledge that more often than not, they're more right than your customers.

Have you ever heard one of those customer service trainers who, without quoting a source, will recycle the old statistic about customers telling four people when they love the service they receive, but telling 10 when they hate it? Maybe it's three if they love it and 11 when they hate it. I don't know — and I don't really care, mostly because that 'truism' is about as true as a barfly tale. But let's assume there's some truth in it. People these days are more cynical than ever, so masters of misery aren't so readily believed when they spread their sad stories.

Just because someone tells me they hate the Greek island of Mykonos is not enough to stop me from flying there to enjoy one of the world's most amazing holiday destinations. I was visiting Mykonos a few years ago when a huge cruise ship stopped there for the day, so for 24 hours the island was bombarded with thousands of additional tourists. It was wonderful. I remember asking two guys who had alighted from the cruise to tell me if they liked it, since I was contemplating doing that very same cruise the following year. Their response was, 'Whatever you do, *do not* go on this cruise. It's terrible! Trust us — you would *hate* it. There's just non-stop parties, all you hear is doof-doof dance music, and you can't get a minute's peace and quiet'. Meanwhile, all I could think was, *where do I sign up!?* So, are potential customers really that lame they'd prefer the advice of a bitter and twisted individual over their own personal likes and dislikes? I think not. And seriously, if your friends just love talking about the different types of customer service they receive, get new friends. You're missing out on some stimulating conversation.

Some customers are bad for your business. Pinpoint these life-suckers and sack them. They make life a misery for your employees, so make them walk the plank into a sea of your competitors. In my late teens, I worked in a call centre and my shift would always finish at 7 pm. If you ever want to see people desperately turning to God, you only need to walk into a call centre 10 minutes before closing time where everyone is praying a call doesn't come through just before their day finishes, because the wrong call at the wrong minute could have them staying back for another hour or more. When there's two minutes to go, call centre operators have their finger poised on the log-off button, ready to disarm the phones the second the clock ticks over to 7 pm.

On one occasion, when there was just one minute remaining to endure, only 60 seconds left to suffer, my phone rang. And all I could remember thinking there were words that would make even a hard-core criminal blush. So I answered the call, spewed my scripted greeting, and in return the very first thing I got in response from the customer was a sinister snarl that slowly and deliberately and loathsomely drawled the following sentence: 'I...hope...you're...not...in...a ...rush...to...go...home...because...you're...going...to ...be...here...for...a...*while*'. And she was right. I was on the phone with this nightmare of a person for the next 90 minutes. If at that point my manager had turned around and mentioned that the customer is always right, I would be writing this book today from a state penitentiary.

Call me a sadist, but for some perverse reason I love receiving poor customer service. When a waitress is too friendly, I find her annoying. But when a waitress is petulant, I find her charming. When a retail assistant is too attentive, I find him meddlesome. But when he's indifferent to my existence, I find him intriguing. Maybe it's the Mediterranean in me, but great customer service just doesn't do it for me. If a store were to open with a tagline of 'the customer is *never* right', I would be there in an instant. And I'm guessing many others would, too. I know I'm in the minority so I'm not suggesting the world should stop providing great customer service. Just don't bang on about it. It's boring.

If this cliché were a product item, it'd be destined for the $2 dustbin. And even then people would return it for their money back. Actually, I saw a great sign in a coffee shop the other day. It read, 'If you are grouchy, irritable, or just plain mean, there will be a $10 charge for putting up with you'. I like the sound of that.

Chapter 23

Under-promise and over-deliver

Imagine a doctor falsely leading you to believe you've contracted tuberculosis but then surprising you with 'Good news, it's just hay fever', jubilant she has another satisfied customer. Or an auto mechanic misinforming you that you'll need a new carburettor but then delighting you by repairing it within the hour, joyful he's been able to 'exceed another client's expectations'. Granted, it would be odd to have a mechanic wanting to exceed a client's expectations, but both of these providers have been manipulative and dishonest by espousing the wow-vow of 'under-promise and over-deliver' that is really underwhelming and overrated.

Here's an idea. Let's just deliver what we promise. The world's most successful brands do exactly that with huge success. No matter which McDonald's store you visit in the world, you know you're always going to receive the same consistent product. They never under-promise and over-deliver by making their Big Mac a Bigger Mac or their Quarter Pounder a Three-Quarter Pounder. When you buy a new house, real estate agents don't throw in a puppy as a way of going 'above and beyond'. They just deliver what they promise. When banks credit your savings account with interest, they don't 'go the extra mile' by throwing in a few extra dollars so you can buy yourself something pretty. They just give you what you signed up for on your application form. Customer relationships should be underpinned by truthfulness and reliability — not undermined by game playing that aims to score brownie points via deception.

Customers' expectations are so high that maybe we should be *over*-promising rather than under-promising. Perhaps it's time to be making daring promises and then finding a way to deliver them. When my publisher agreed to release this book, I boldly over-promised a deadline of six weeks to write 50 000 words, when it usually takes me two days to write just 1000. I was determined to deliver, so this became my plan: (a) I cut out all social activities, making me lonelier than the time I went on a couples-only sunset cruise that wouldn't have been so bad had I not been on my own (Loser!); (b) I stopped going to the gym, when doing so this close to summer was a greater threat to my social life than Step A and (c) I stopped reading newspapers, which to a current affairs addict is like trying to wrestle chocolate from the mouth of a spoilt fat child. If you're reading this in February 2010, I met the deadline. If it's now after that date, you might be my editor reading it as a Word document and you hate my guts. The 'under-promise and over-deliver' cliché seeks to promise and promote the ordinary. I'm not sure that's good for branding.

Is the above sustainable? No, but it was never going to be forever. It's just what had to be done to achieve an over-promise. What's really unsustainable is to continually beat expectations because the constant exceeding of those expectations will become the new expectation. When I was a middle manager managing a large team, I wanted to build a people-focused reputation, so I dedicated an hour a day to walking around the floor chatting with each staff member. Initially, I could see scepticism in their eyes and sense awkwardness in their guise, but after a while they became relaxed and I began to get comments such as, 'A manager of your level has never even spoken to us before'. I was immensely proud I was exceeding their expectations ... until the exceeding of those expectations became their expectation. If on a particular day I was so busy that I'd cut out that hour of social time, I'd get resentful comments such as, 'Don't you like us anymore?' On some days, I'd just innocently forget to do it, and so I'd overhear remarks such as, 'Stay away from James today, guys. He's cracked it'. I achieved my mission of being people-focused at the expense of flexibility in my delivery. I still continued with the walk-around because the expectation had now been set, and to be honest, it was my favourite part of the day. But what I learnt was that a consistent surprise stops being surprising.

If you under-promise too much, it makes it harder to win a customer's business when you're competing with others who are willing to do whatever it takes. It's like going to a convenience store and inconveniently finding the front door locked with a sign saying, 'Back in five minutes'. Just the other day I came across one of those signs, so I thought, fine, I'll wait five minutes. But then 10 minutes went by and still the shopkeeper hadn't arrived. So I figured since I'd waited 10 minutes already, I may as well wait another five. Before I knew it, 15 minutes had passed and that's when the guy finally dawdled back in from the toilet, placing the magazine he must have been reading on the toilet back on the newsstand. If the sign in the window had under-promised by saying, 'Back in 20 minutes', there's no way I would have waited. I would have walked off in a huff and puff a few blocks down the road to a more convenient convenience store muttering that time is far too precious to waste waiting. Yes, the shopkeeper broke the cardinal rule of not delivering what was promised, but this is just an example of the comparative impact of over-promising versus under-promising. By promising too little, you risk being disqualified by potential customers.

Exceeding customers' expectations can actually be counterproductive. Instead of making them feel pleased, your actions can create unease. You can see this happening on the stock market. When a company unexpectedly announces a colossal profit way beyond what was initially predicted, the market response is often negative because astute investors start to question how an organisation was able to get the forecast so wrong. They become suspicious and suspenseful, nervous the instability and volatility could just as quickly result in a reversal of that fortune.

On a smaller scale, you can see this within marriages. If over the past decade a husband hasn't told his wife he loves her, hasn't taken her out for a romantic dinner and hasn't bought her any cute surprises, it's fair enough for the wife to think King Vidor was right — marriage isn't a word; it's a sentence. But then if all of a sudden the husband turns into a romping Romeo, what's the first thought that's likely to enter the wife's mind? 'He's having an affair!'

As Norman Vincent Peale once said, 'Promises are like crying babies in a theatre — they should be carried out at once'.

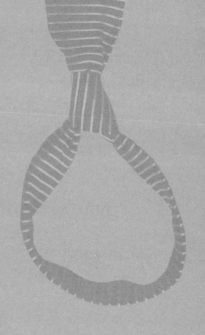

Part VI

Teach for the stars

Chapter 24

Knowledge is power

I'm a university dropout. Some of you reading this will be disgusted. In your eyes I've lost all credibility by admitting that one truth. You're tempted to stop reading because you feel cheated, dirty, used. All this time you've been thinking these words have been borne from the brain of a learned individual, not some uneducated know-it-all who was raised near the drive-by shooting capital of Australia. Regardless, I voluntarily dropped out of university three-quarters of the way into my business degree. I think I'm still in denial. Whenever I get asked to complete random consumer surveys, I tick the demographic box marked 'university graduate' in the education section. Settling for 'secondary education' is just too humiliating. Apart from being so bored I could chew on a limb and still be restless, the primary reason I departed university was because I wasn't convinced of the usefulness or practicality of what I was learning. In essence, knowledge had stopped giving me power.

If knowledge is power, then surely university professors would be the richest and most successful people on the planet. After all, their brains are full of foolproof knowledge. Crammed with research and data, their powerful minds resemble the ancient Greek city of Sparta, armoured and armed with studies, journals and white papers. Instead, many of them work in cramped offices, drive old cars and wear clothes that were in fashion back in the days when it was still cool to do 'The Hustle'. If knowledge is power, people such as George W Bush wouldn't have become president of the United States. Irrespective of whether you agree or disagree with his politics, there's no denying the lack of knowledge in a man who says things such as, 'So long as I'm the president, my measure of success is victory — and success'.

I'd like to put it to you that knowledge can actually create *powerlessness*, rather than power. As an example, take swine flu. It wasn't too long ago the world was gripped by the man-made hysteria that I like to call 'whine flu' — because the whole thing was really just one big whinge. During the few months that whine flu had the attention of the media, a few hundred people died of its complications. Compare that to the number of people who died during the same period from the normal flu (about 50 000), and you start to get some perspective on how the knowledge of whine flu fuelled a frenzy of fear in every country in which it reared its pig-like head.

Similarly, the global financial crisis didn't have to be as severe as what it turned out to be. But the never-ending knowledge of bad news perpetuated in the media did nothing but crush consumer confidence and propel employers into a petrified panic. It was only when people started becoming bored of hearing about it that things slowly started to turn around. I'm not saying that knowledge is bad. It's enriching. It's vital. But does it create more powerlessness than power? Time and again, yes, it does.

Fundamentally, knowledge is not enough to attain power. What a person needs to snatch a patch of power is a little something called … talent. I could read every book on boxing, memorise every punching technique and record every boxing match to watch and re-watch, yet no amount of analysing, no amount of learning and no amount of knowledge acquisition can make up for the fact I punch like a cheerleader, more worried about scratching my moisturised hand than I am about inflicting pain on my opponent. Despite the knowledge a person absorbs, a lack of talent will always hold them back from being able to clutch the much-vaunted value of power.

So if knowledge is not power, then what is power? *Understanding* is power. It's one thing to have a library of textbooks ingrained in your brain, but it's another to truly comprehend them. It's one thing to recite a complex algorithm, but it's another to really grasp the truth behind it. It's one thing to know the intricacies of a process, but it's another to totally appreciate the causes and reasons for why it exists. Knowledge provides you with the foundation. Understanding rewards you with the power. Many people are just equipped with the facts. That's all. No understanding. Just facts.

They're like my old scripture teacher in primary school. She knew all about Adam and Eve. She was well-versed with the psalms. She was familiar with the church protocols. (It was she that taught me sternly it wasn't appropriate to bang on a confessional door just for a laugh while someone was in there sincerely revealing their sins to an eager priest. The poor sinner thought it was God sending her a sign.) She knew the rights and wrongs, the hymns and the songs, but despite all of the Bible-esque information she possessed, she had little *real understanding* of her subject matter. She would flutter and flail whenever I'd ask her a question that required her to dig into her *understanding* of the topic in order to answer it. For example, the one query she could never answer for me was, 'If Jesus is the answer — then what is the question?' If she had been able to use her understanding rather than her knowledge, perhaps she would've had greater influence over my life. Instead, my eight-year-old classmates and I would use her class to stray more than we'd pray.

Power is also *action*. The definitive case of people who don't get this point can be seen at personal development events. They're called 'seminar junkies' and they act like leeches. They hang around at motivational symposiums and educational conventions like an ageing relative that just won't die. They'll attend everything — every course, every conference, every coaching session. Years go by and you still see them going to the same types of events run by the same types of sages who all continue to say the same thing. And yet they're at an identical spot today as when they started their 'journey' 10 years ago. They take copious amounts of notes and get sucked into exorbitantly priced advanced programs, while the organiser uses a leg to kick them up the arse and a hand to steal their wallet. They rarely do anything with what they've learnt. They have enough knowledge. They know all they need to know. Their problem isn't one of information but one of action.

The information age has changed how we communicate, how we socialise, how we learn, how we buy and how we sell. We've been put under its spell, but it's time we moved on to the next stage of evolution. The in-formation age, perhaps?

Chapter 25

Every mistake is a learning experience

It's been a delight smashing the management clichés throughout this book. The process has been therapeutic as I've bashed out on the keyboard what I wish I'd lashed out to my managers. But this particular cliché, about learning from every mistake, makes me feel merciless because I know there are people reading this who've screwed up in the past but have passed it off as a learning experience, and now they're about to see that, no, it was still just a screw-up. This cliché is the perfect thing to say to your employees to make them feel better about their underperformance. But just between you and me, if every mistake was really a learning experience, by now the extent of my education would have resulted in letters after my name instead of a question mark. For example, rather than overhearing 'Is his surname really

Adonis?' I would catch whispers of, 'Wow, James Adonis MD MBA LMNOP'.

The people inclined to look at every mistake as a learning experience are those who regrettably say 'I have no regrets'. Well, none that they care to admit. There's an Australian magazine that profiles a high-profile CEO every week. One of the questions the CEOs are asked is 'Do you have any regrets?' Most say they don't, and considering the average age of these corporate leaders is 50, it makes me wonder if they're (a) lying, (b) narcissists or (c) not trying hard enough.

If they're *lying*, they probably assume confessing to a mishap stains their reputation, when in reality it's more inspiring to have leaders who are open about their misfortunes. For example, I regret the time I ran my first ever public seminar, which was coincidentally also my debut presentation to an audience. Tragically, I had forgotten to book the meeting room. When I arrived at the venue, I was told they were fully booked. Noticing the weepy tremble of my bottom lip, they kindly put me up in their staff kitchen. But this wasn't just *any* kitchen. This was an old 1950s relic, with dirty dishes piled up like the Leaning Tower of Pisa; bric-a-brac stacked around like a garbage tip; chairs with broken legs and torn padding for my paying guests to sit on, or rather, to balance on, and staff members walking in to make coffee as I delivered a public presentation for the first time in my life. I regret that none of the companies in attendance became clients. I regret that the people in the audience will forever remember me as the guy who got so nervous he choked on his own words and had to dive for a bottle of water. I regret that the bottle of water wasn't mine but someone else's in the front row. I've accepted the regrets, dealt with them and have since moved on. See, it's not such a big deal.

If they're *narcissists*, it means they've got such a low level of self-awareness they wouldn't even recognise Regret if it came up and introduced itself wearing nothing but a shirt saying, 'It's better to regret someone you did than someone you didn't'.

And if they're *not trying* hard enough, it's because they've spent a lifetime playing it safe, and so perhaps for them every mistake should be a yearning experience instead of a learning one.

This cliché means well. That part is obvious. But some mistakes are so disastrous it's hard for them to be learning experiences. What if someone accidentally kills a colleague at work? 'Oops, sorry about that, boss. It won't happen again. But it's cool. I've learnt my lesson now.' Or you might recall the bank employee who unintentionally transferred $10 million into a customer's account, with the customer fleeing the country shortly after. I imagine the employee would have sounded a little like Steve Urkel, 'Did I do thaaaaaat?' What if an employee's erratic and erroneous behaviour results in an entire company collapse? It's inconceivable that the individual's supervisor would have a chat with him about what he's learnt from the experience and to 'brainstorm what he'd do differently in the future'. Nope, some mistakes are simply that. Stupid, stupid mistakes.

Instead of learning from our mistakes, we learn best from our successes. This was highlighted by research conducted by MIT in 2009, which showed that brain cells learn better from positive experiences than they do from negative ones. Their study proved that there's a greater chance of repeating certain behaviours when we do them correctly than there is in avoiding behaviours when we do them wrong. You can see this most prominently in our schooling system. Students do well in classes that are aligned with their natural talents and strengths, while they struggle in classes at which they'll never have the right aptitude.

When I was at school, I would consistently get into trouble for talking in class, resulting in after-school detention on most Friday afternoons. One teacher in particular would snidely comment that I could fit seven semitrailers in my mouth sideways underwater and still be able to hold a conversation. Yet despite repeated detentions and defeated intentions, I didn't change my behaviour. More often than not, this would occur in classes like woodwork and metalwork which are such an anathema to my personality I would ask my dad to complete my assignments. I wish I could have preserved the look of astonishment on my teachers' faces when the kid who couldn't even saw a piece of wood in half would rock up with a homemade remote-control car that was so good it could be sold in department stores. But then there were other classes where I'd be as silent as a mute's whisper and more attentive than a peeping Tom. Classes like English, Drama and History were so aligned with my interests, values, talents and strengths that I just couldn't fail. I learnt far more from the successes I had with the classes where I excelled than the mistakes I encountered with the classes where I bombed. And this isn't just me, but everyone who focuses more on their successes than their mistakes.

Even the biggest fanatics of this cliché would admit that as much as people would love to learn from their mistakes, it frequently doesn't happen. For some reason, we foolishly keep repeating them. Despite vowing to never have a fat summer again, many of us continue to eat like pigs even while spring is springing away. Despite having our tongues burnt on more than one occasion, we continue to sip from a hot cup of coffee before it's cooled down. And despite swearing to never again humiliate ourselves when intoxicated, we continue to make drunken phone calls to our ex-partners, confessing to what we'd never say when we're sober. I *wish* we learnt from our mistakes.

Chapter 26

There's no such thing as a stupid question

You must have been in a learning environment at some stage where upon an audience member asking a question, the facilitator's response began with, 'Thanks, that's a really good question'. Even when the question is about as welcome as incontinence, facilitators still feel compelled to credit the questioner as if they've just volunteered the meaning of life. On many occasions I've wanted to ask the facilitator what it was in particular they found so good about that last question, but I refrain. Instead, I patiently sit through sessions where participants are told 'There's no such thing as a stupid question', which just encourages them to avoid thinking before speaking. To kill this cliché once and for all, here are the six most common types of stupid questions many of us are assaulted with on a daily basis.

The stating-the-obvious questions

These are questions where the answer is so clear, so apparent, the questioner must have been lost in an Amazonian jungle for 30 years to not know the answer. Questions in this category include:

⇒ 'How often do the monthly mentoring sessions occur?' Um, monthly.

⇒ 'It's a hot day today, isn't it?' Yes, it must be the weather.

⇒ 'Are they your kids in that photo?' No, they're my next-door neighbour's, but I just like to keep them on my desk. Don't ask me why.

The getting-off-track questions

These are annoying for their sheer irrelevance. They're usually asked midway through a story, thereby interrupting the plot's flow. Perpetrators will throw their question in like a spear piercing the heart of its victim just as the climax or punch line is about to be revealed. Getting-off-track questions serve no purpose. At work, they don't enhance the group's knowledge. They don't elevate the level of comprehension. All they do is detract from the topic and waste precious time. Questions in this category include:

⇒ 'How *is* Tom, anyway?' (Often asked by people who hear a familiar name during a monologue and feel the uncontrollable urge to interrupt immediately to find out about the welfare of said individual.)

⇒ 'Oh my God, can I tell you about how that *exact* same thing happened to me in my last job, only better?' (This question is usually impatiently asked even before your story has finished, in which case the only logical retort is, 'How does 'no' sound? Is 'no' good for you?')

⇒ 'It's always the way, isn't it?' No, it's not. That's why it's a *story*.

The of-course questions

These are favourites with conference leaders who, in their attempts to incorporate 'audience interaction' into their presentations, will chuck the of-course questions in there which do nothing but patronise their audience. Of-course questions are superfluous because only an idiot would answer in the negative. Questions in this category include:

⇒ 'Are you all having a good time so far? I can't hear you! I said, are you all having a good time so far?' Not anymore, bozo.

⇒ 'Hands up who wants more money! Hands up who wants to be happier! Hands up who wants better relationships!' Hands up who wants to get the hell away from condescending questions disguised as statements!

⇒ 'James, let me ask you a serious question. You want to increase your sales, right?' No, I want you out of my office. (The only appropriate response to such a skin-crawling question asked by many salespeople.)

The too-bloody-lazy questions

These are asked by assailants who can't be bothered looking up the answer. It's much easier for them to ask someone else and is often preceded by 'I'm sorry to be a pain, but…' In most cases, during the time it took them to ask their question, they could have discovered the answer for themselves. But this thought would never occur to them since their specialty is to ask too-bloody-lazy questions, I presume just for the sake of asking one. Questions in this category include:

⇒ 'My computer is experiencing Error R307. What does that mean?' Look it up in the help guide. You'll find the answer in the 'user problems' section, with emphasis on the word 'user'.

⇒ 'How am I meant to put this new desk together?' You know that piece of paper with the pictures that came in the box? The one called 'instructions'?

⇒ 'can u txt me ur email pls coz lunch is now 2mro? k? dont be l8! lol. thx cya' (Even though it's somewhat different to the other two questions, this one fits within this category because the questioners are too lazy to find out the information for themselves. Then they add insult to injury by slaughtering the English language by writing in 'textese'.)

The plain-old-dumb questions

If your response is 'Did she just say that?' or 'Is he being serious?', then you've probably been asked a plain-old-dumb question. Out of all the stupid questions, these are the most stupid. Questions in this category include the following, all three of which I've been asked over the past month:

⇒ 'Is Asia a country?'

⇒ 'Is that in lower case?' (When referring to my website URL.)

⇒ 'How do you spell that?' (Err, J – A – M – E – S.)

The what-did-you-just-say questions

These are questions put forward so inarticulately that it's unlikely even the questioner understands what's being asked. You can seek clarification three times and still be baffled. In response, nod your head, smile and say something so vague it can't be wrong. Something like, 'The answer is yes and no. It really depends on the situation and the finer details. Any other questions?' Questions in this category include the following:

⇒ 'Is your theory of management egalitarian, say, with decentralised affiliates where interconnected silos that aren't strategising but are coherently regulated form, some would say, catharsis and indemnity?'

⇒ 'But what if that thing doesn't correlate with the other thing especially when that one is without the other, you know what I mean?'

⇒ 'Callaban youlouboo pallabese relebeat thalabat forlobor melebee?'

I saw written on a T-shirt recently: *There is no such thing as a stupid question. Only stupid people.* That almost makes me want to embrace this cliché. Almost. In the meantime, to say there's no such thing as a stupid question is, quite frankly, stupid.

Part VII

Hook, line
and thinker

Chapter 27

Think outside the box

Most often associated with creativity, managers encourage their employees to think outside the box so that new ideas are unwrapped, unique solutions are unpacked and original thoughts are released from a security-complex of staleness. Usually held in brainstorming sessions, employees are asked to contribute any suggestions 'no matter how wacky or out-there' knowing full well the wacky and out-there ideas will be disregarded because they're wacky and out-there.

The irony with the 'think outside the box' cliché is that it's declared so many times by wannabe inspirers the phrase itself has become *inside*-the-box thinking. When managers try to motivate their staff to think creatively by saying something as uncreative as 'think outside the box', they're demonstrating their own inability to do so themselves. It's just like giving someone fashion advice when you're dressed like a fortune-teller. It's not believable.

A problem with thinking outside the box is that you're ignoring the box. The box represents the fundamentals and the constraints. It represents what's possible and what's not. It represents what you and others have learnt in the past and what remains untapped. How can you think outside the box if you don't know what it looks like? I see this whenever I engage in political debates with people who don't know much about politics. When I was at school, while the other kids were looking forward to turning 18 so they could drink alcohol, go to nightclubs and drive on their own, I looked forward to being 18 so I could vote. There isn't a single topic in the world that gets me more passionate than to discuss the intricacies of foreign policy, the rights and wrongs of the left and the right and the most exciting night of the year (besides the Eurovision Song Contest) when an election night is on.

I tell you this because everything I've read and experienced about politics is the box which represents the fundamentals and constraints, the possible and the impossible, the past and the present. So when I have debates with those holding an opposite and ignorant view, those who think outside the box without consideration of the box, I struggle to stay sane because the conversation is not based on reality. I've got a beautiful friend I adore who's convinced the world should eradicate money and revert to a bartering system; who fervently believes war is not necessary even if your country is being attacked and who thinks if everyone in the world just meditated at the same time, we'd be free of the ills plaguing our planet. Her extreme solutions characterise out-of-the-box thinking. Would her ideas be lovely in an ideal world? Perhaps. Are they possible? No, they're about as impossible as Barbie's waistline. In the end, thinking outside the box sends us spiralling into an abyss where we become exasperated at the gap between what is and what could be.

Sometimes you might look at an ingeniously creative person and compliment them on their ability to think outside the box, when really they're simply thinking inside the box of a totally separate construct — a different box, so to speak. To that other person on whose head we place the think-outside-the-box crown, the answer to whatever conundrum they're solving is obvious to them because it's based on the data and know-how they've acquired over the years.

Madonna is a case in point. If there were ever to be an entertainer who could be credited for furthering the think-outside-the-box cause, it would be Ms Ciccone. Decades after she first fired up the music scene, Madonna is still scoring number one hits all over the world and making more money than her long-forgotten contemporaries who have a greater chance of mountain-climbing in Jimmy Choos than seeing the summit of another chart-topper. No-one of her generation, in fact, no-one of any generation, is able to compare with her ability to reinvent and reinvigorate. She once said, 'I sometimes think I was born to live up to my name. How could I be anything else but what I am having been named Madonna? I would either have ended up a nun or this'. It seems as though she's thinking outside the box, but really she's just being herself. She's sitting in a different box rather than thinking outside of one.

Here's a quick task for you. Take a few seconds to think of as many items as you can that are rectangular in shape. If you're like me, you'll ignore the instruction and continue reading. I'm cool with that. I wouldn't do it, either. Whenever an author makes a request for the completion of an exercise in a book, I always disregard it and head straight for the point. 'I haven't got time for this', I muse. 'Just tell me what

I need to know.' Okay, so let's continue to pretend you're doing what I'm asking. I'd like you to note down as many things in the *world* that are in the shape of a rectangle. You have 15 seconds to do so. Now I'd like you to write down all of the rectangular-shaped items that can be found in a *house*. Again, you have 15 seconds. Compare the two lists. Chances are you wrote down more rectangular items the second time around than the first even though there are obviously more rectangular items in the whole world than in a small house. This is because the parameters in place when you think *inside* the box enable you to produce a better outcome by focusing intently on the surroundings most familiar to you. To think outside the box is to remove the boundaries which ordinarily act like guiding lampposts.

Let's assume it's good to think outside the box. You get your employees together, you tell them you want to increase profits and ask for their suggestions. The whiteboard begins to fill with painfully predictable terms like economies of scale, cost-benefit analysis and due diligence. People nod around the boardroom table. The loud one keeps talking over people so he's seen to be the greatest thinker. The quiet one, who's actually doing the thinking, still hasn't said anything. And before you know it, you have a final agenda of addenda to add to the job responsibilities of an already overworked workforce. Stretched beyond their limits with no additional resources to help them cope, eventually your well-meaning meeting has manifested a tedious to-do list, none of which gets done and all of which leads to moribund morale when expectations are crushed and targets missed. That's what outside-the-box thinking does. It's there not because it's been proven to work in the past, but because it's become such an ingrained part of the management lexicon that lax leaders keep reciting it. How 'creative'.

Thinking outside the box just isn't what it's cut out to be.

Chapter 28

Perception is reality

If I'm wrong about this one, if perception really is reality, then I'm screwed. Because that would mean I'm an inconsiderate pig with the kindest heart; the world's worst friend and a soul mate to many; a cynical pessimist beaming with eternal optimism; a good-for-nothing loser that's an inspirational success; and a right-wing fascist obsessed about human rights. It all depends on who you ask, of course. Nevertheless, it seems I've been busy. So if perception is in fact reality, that means I suffer from multiple personality disorder, in which case I'd like to introduce you to my other selves: 'don't care' and 'still don't care'.

It defies belief that people would accept as synonyms two words that are relative opposites. Perception is perception, and reality is reality. The notion behind this cliché is you are what others think you are. Their perception might be steeped in inaccuracy, but if that's what they think then that's what you are. It ignores what's right and sides with the delusional, and it abandons reason and supports the misguided. Reality is the truth. Perception, when it differs from that truth, is a falsehood.

I live across the road from a homeless shelter. There's a guy who sits on the front turf, and whenever I walk past him he aggressively yells at me, 'It's *you*, ya little bastard! Gotcha!' and chases me around the block, presumably trying to kill me. Now, in his mind, I am unmistakably a little bastard. In fact, his perception of me as a little bastard is so crystal clear that he feels the need to pursue me in a fit of rage throughout the streets of Sydney's red light district, motivated by the thought of his hands gripping tightly around my neck. Is his perception of me the truth? No, it's not. I've never met the guy before, let alone in a capacity to have been cruel, and so to resign myself to the fallacy that perception is reality just doesn't make sense. His perception is not the reality, and so I shouldn't accept it.

The predicament that pops up when you're an enthusiast of this cliché is you begin to manage by perception. You start to rely too much on what other people think, and your self-esteem hinges on whether they love you or hate you. When you're adored, you're walking on air. But when you're disliked, you're walking in despair. Your happiness ends up being dependent on the assessments others have of you — even when those assessments are erroneous. This incessant seeking of self-aggrandisement is most evident in politicians, where our members of parliament will go to extraordinary lengths to be perceived as doing an excellent job, otherwise known as 'spin doctoring'. In 2009 the Australian government announced the nation was going to record a deficit in the billions of dollars. Compared to other countries around the world, this was no big deal. But when the prime minister was interviewed in the media about the state of the budget, he refused to mention the word 'billion', thinking that by avoiding the term altogether, Australians will be oblivious to what's going on. Here's an edited transcript from an interview with journalist Tony Jones on the ABC's *Lateline* program. My comments are in brackets.

> TONY JONES: What's the peak figure of the projected public debt in terms of tens or hundreds of billions of dollars in the coming years? What's the peak figure?

> PM: Well, these are clearly outlined in the Budget papers and they're usually expressed in terms of a percentage of GDP. We peak, in around about 2013, at about 13.8 per cent of GDP.

> TONY JONES: How much of that is in tens of billions or hundreds of billions of dollars; how much is that?

> PM: Well, let me step back in terms of the elements of this. First of all, 70 per cent of our overall position here is determined by a $214 billion collapse in tax revenue. That's one slice of it.

> TONY JONES: OK. I understand — we understand that. So what is the figure of peak debt in hundreds of billions of dollars? What is the actual figure?

> PM: Well, Tony, I'm about to come to that when I go to constituent parts. *(The Prime Minister goes on to talk extensively about a collapse in tax revenues again and other spending initiatives, but avoids the question as if it's his wife asking him if her bum looks big in this.)*

> TONY JONES: But all I'm asking for is one figure.

> PM: Well, I'm about to come to that, Tony. I'm taking you to the constituent parts. *(The Prime Minister starts*

talking about the percentage again before kind-of admitting the final figure among a whole lot of other data.)

TONY JONES: That figure is $300 billion, is that right?

PM: As I said before, 13.8 per cent of GDP as described accurately in the budget papers. There's nothing new about that.

TONY JONES: Is there a political spin rule which says the prime minister must not say that figure? Because it seems very hard to get you to say $300 billion.

And on it goes. It was more excruciating to watch than a marathon screening of David Hasselhoff music videos, and yet this charade was repeated on several occasions over a number of days. It did far more damage to the perception of the government simply because the government's infatuation with that perception was so obvious. All it did was place the spotlight on the very figure the prime minister was trying to avoid. He assumed by leaving out the word 'billion' nobody would notice the budget was now in the red. Instead, he went red in the face all because he was trying to manage the *perception* rather than the *reality*.

Perception does not matter. Reality does. And yet it's perception so many people prioritise with prying eyes. The stock market is a perfect example of the perception versus reality argument. The share price of any given company is primarily based on perception. The price is driven up the more that people perceive it to have potential, and the price is driven down whenever it's perceived to have an unstable future. But the reality, however, is a different story. A publicly listed company might be doing enormously well in terms of its share price, but if under the radar there is fraud, embezzlement, illegal practices or a host of any other white-collar crimes, the public often doesn't find out until it's too late. Companies like HIH and Enron are cases in point where the focus on perception disguised the unfortunate reality.

I'll give you a more personal example. Whenever I facilitate training sessions, I never provide the participants with feedback sheets for them to rate the day, because it's not important whether they perceive me to be funny or serious, and I have very little care factor on their perception of the catering or the temperature of the air conditioning. All I'm concerned about is one aspect: has the purpose of the day been achieved? If they're thinking differently, speaking differently and acting differently as a result of the workshop, then my mission has been accomplished. The rest is perceptive irrelevance. One person's thoughts about the venue could be markedly different to another's, while one participant's taste for the background music might be dissimilar to someone else's. In my early days, when I thought feedback sheets were a given, one guy wrote in the 'comments' section: 'You're a natural. Great day. But the next time we catch up, remind me to give you some feedback about your hair and your clothes'. Yep, thanks. If I paid attention to this perceptive nonsense, I'd go crazy.

The closest perception comes to reality is if you were to rephrase this cliché to read perception is *a* reality. When someone is exceptionally strong-minded, their view of the world is so resolute that very little can be done to change it. In their mind, the truth is the truth and there's nothing you can do about it. One of my recent blog posts was on the topic of 'Why do women earn less than men?' Out of the 104 comments by readers, here is my favourite one, not at all because I agree with this sour man but solely due to it making me chuckle that people could hold such a stern and steadfast stance: 'Men are smarter, faster, stronger (both mentally and physically) and dealing with female coworkers (especially in an office environment) is worse than dealing with diabetes'. Lovely, isn't he? When you come across people like this in real life, you need to re-evaluate how much energy you invest in trying to change such an enforced perception, especially when it's clearly untrue.

There are some clichés in this book that can be used as an abuse of power. This is one of them. I'll explain. Have you ever been on dates with people who are so besotted with you that you could say anything to them, absolutely anything, and they'll agree with you? They're so imposingly trying to impress that they'll concur just so that you think highly of them. It's such a pity because they're so blinded by lust they actually believe what they're nodding their heads to. It's far more admirable when people stand up and defend their beliefs, but that doesn't include the meek 'let's agree to disagree' line, which just reeks of weakness. No, let's not 'agree to disagree'! Stand up and fight! So, occasionally when I go on dates, which to be fair is quite rare, I'll test the people I'm with on the strength of their conviction. I'll lay out a claim so preposterous, so insanely absurd, that to agree would be akin to declaring on national TV their dad's sexy. I've had people agreeing to bigoted and extreme positions on racism, sexism, violence and more, which shows the abuse of power this cliché potentially holds. This is because the person with the strongest character, the individual with the greatest influence, the master with the superior authority, can declare a perception to be a reality at any time, and by force or manipulation get others to embrace that perception as a fact. Objectivity is out. Subjectivity is in.

I don't think so. Not in my reality.

Chapter 29

To assume makes an ass out of U and me

I'm going to start this chapter with a few assumptions. I assume you've mentioned this cliché at some stage during your career. I assume you think it's true. I assume, therefore, that it's useful to read this alternative perspective, which argues that assumptions are more of an asset than an ass. Whoever came up with this clever mocking phrase must have been hurt by assumptions in the past, but that in itself is not enough of a reason to condemn assumptions to the bowels of business. Yes, assumptions can sometimes be dangerous, but mostly they serve you well. To banish them due to previous unfortunate experiences is like deciding to put your baby up for adoption just because it cries. It's like ruling out baths just because the water goes cold. It's ... dare I say it ... *throwing the baby out with the bathwater.*

The first harmless assumptions are *best-case* ones. These are when you assume the best in people. It's called 'being a nice person'. Instead of living in a state of consternation that they might do wrong by you, best-case assumptions give new relationships the finest opportunity to work without poisoning them with negative thoughts from the onset. When you pre-judge and worry over how people will treat you in the future, you risk turning that fear into a reality. That's why our justice system is based on the principle of 'innocent until proven guilty'. Jurors are asked to assume the defendant's innocence, to assume the best, and to let the evidence sway them either way.

When I was 19, I was the jury foreman on a drug dealing trial. After only the very first day, before we'd even heard much of the evidence, one of my fellow jurors, an elderly man in a wheelchair, openly declared the defendant was guilty. 'I've already decided he's guilty and that's that', he snapped aggressively. We were all taken aback. By making such an unfair assumption, this guy was setting the defendant up for failure. I mean, sure, the defendant was caught with drugs in his diary, he'd frantically bolted away from the cops as they approached and he looked about as innocent as OJ Simpson, but that's beside the point. In the end, it was a hung jury, and it didn't help our deliberations that there were jurors who'd reached a conclusion before the conclusion. By drawing attention to what you dread, you dredge up what you resent.

In the same way best-case assumptions come in handy, so do *worst-case* ones. When planning a project, it's best to assume the worst in regards to time so inconvenient delays don't occur. When launching a new business, it's best to assume the worst in terms of start-up costs, so you're not left penniless when you need it most. When purchasing insurance, it's best to assume the worst so you're adequately covered no matter what happens. It's just like Greek family dinners. My incredible mother, who is the consummate cook, will always assume the worst when it comes to catering. If she's cooking for a group of 10, she'll always make enough food to feed 100.

It's perfectly okay to make assumptions so long as you're open about them. You'll notice when companies put in for big tenders, they'll usually include a section titled 'Assumptions' where they outline what the quote depends upon from the client's perspective. Assumptions only become perilous when they're kept hidden, such as in false advertising. Organisations promote their products by implicitly promising wealth, beauty, coolness and a range of other desires when their hidden assumption is you'll believe all that stuff is within reach. I bought a book a while ago called *Six-Pack Abs in Six Weeks*. It's been six months and I'm still stuck with just one abdominal muscle. The authors of that book have made a couple of hidden assumptions. The first is they must surely know it's unrealistic for most people to get a six-pack within six weeks, but it's a manipulative marketing tool that gets desperate people like me to buy the book. And the second hidden assumption is those of us dissatisfied with the results would be too lazy to get off our fat arses and take the book back for a refund. It's not the fact that assumptions exist that's the problem, but rather that they're hidden. That's what creates the fairytale high hopes and the ultimate displeasure.

You can't avoid making assumptions in business. It's not possible to see everything, to validate everything or to conduct a thorough analysis prior to every decision. On many occasions you just have to rely on your gut instinct — on an assumption. It's like driving a car. Everyone knows a road is full of hazards that cause car crashes. It's not possible for us to predict them all. You can't see the entire road ahead so that you know what hazards will come your way. You just confidently step on the accelerator and drive off with the assumption you'll be alright — unless, of course, you're Thelma and Louise. Your challenge is to then have a process in place that ensures your assumptions are as safe as possible. That's much wiser than ruling out assumptions altogether. This process can include evaluating the success of your assumptions from the past; involving others by seeking their feedback; having a system in place that detects when your assumptions go astray and anything else that reduces the level of risk.

It's outrageous assumptions that have stimulated the greatest progress in society. JFK made a bold assumption when he said a man would be on the moon by the end of the decade. Barack Obama made a visionary assumption that a grassroots campaign would get him elected as America's first black president. Gandhi made an audacious assumption he could overthrow the British Empire using peaceful methods. Instead, the nature of corporate life is such that the most outrageous characters with the most shocking ideas become ostracised for being so outlandish. They're not revered like JFK or admired like Barack Obama or respected like Gandhi. They're demonised for being different and put down for being peculiar. They're the nerdy kid at school without friends who got ignored until his peers saw with regret he became the owner of a company called Microsoft. Or it's the unattractive tall girl in class with the braces who was teased until her peers saw with regret she became the world's first supermodel. They're ignored like the creepy drunken uncle at a Christmas party who keeps looking at you funny. We pretend they're not there, even though it's the wackiest people making the most daring assumptions we should be paying attention to the most.

To disregard assumptions is in effect making an assumption. See the irony?

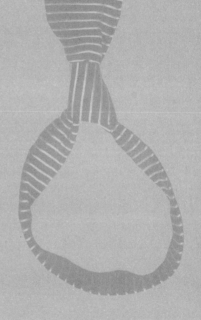

Part VIII

Tickle the money bone

Chapter 30

Time is money, money is time

My entire life I've always wanted to be a millionaire by 30. Well, I'm writing this chapter a few weeks before my 30th birthday. A wise friend once told me you should never be afraid of getting older. The only time you should dread getting older is when you haven't achieved the goals you'd hoped to achieve by that time. Well, folks, that's me. I don't mind turning 30. But I do mind that I've reluctantly had to accept that there's a bigger chance the Republican Party will choose a black ghetto-lesbian porn-star atheist welfare-dependant single mother-of-five to be their presidential candidate before I'm able to reach my lifelong goal. As a result of relentlessly chasing this ambition, I've tripped into the quicksand that is this cliché. I've sacrificed social time for work time, given up holidays for workdays and turned weekends into backbends. And it's only now I've realised anyone who believes time is money and money is time really needs some time out.

I love money, and I still want to be a multimillionaire, although if you were to have seen my credit card debt in the past, you would have advised me to scale down my financial desires to something a little more achievable, like being solvent. Nevertheless, I tell you this because I don't want you to think I've turned into a money-hating socialist. I've learnt that if I lose my money, I can get it back. But if I lose time with people I love, I can't. I know that sounds sappier than a Hallmark card, but I've learnt that what differentiates me from the rich might be the number of zeros in my bank balance, but what doesn't differentiate me is the number of hours in my day. So to say time is money and money is time is to put the two on an equal footing. It's to assume time spent not making money is time wasted. As a result, we become like Scrooge McDuck where mounting pennies become more important than counting memories.

Time, which is intangible, can't possibly be money, which is tangible. If time is going to be anything at all, it needs to be something intrinsic to you, whatever you choose for that to be. Maybe time to you is life, which is the amount of living you squeeze into it. Perhaps time to you is charity, which is the amount of giving you fit into it. Or time to you might be work, which is the amount of striving you push into it. Time can be the heart and the soul, the rhythm and a whole lot of goals, but one thing it's not is a bankroll. There have been plenty of periods when I've had enough money to live on happily ever after ... so long as I didn't eat, drink or make any purchases. And it was during those times I would need to constantly fight the Spike Milligan in me who would wistfully beg to a higher power, 'All I ask is the chance to *prove* that money can't make me happy!' Money can buy you fancy cars, expensive cigars and a dose of plastic surgery, but it can't get you any more time.

If time is money and money is time, there wouldn't be consultants refusing to charge clients by the hour for their services. Instead, their fees are commensurate with the difference they make. If they save the company $10 million, they ask for 5 per cent. If they increase revenues by orchestrating a merger, their contract demands a slice of the splice. When clever entrepreneurs build their businesses, they create scalable models so a boost in income doesn't necessarily mean a single additional hour needs to be worked. In comparison, those who view time as being equal to money end up sweating for every dollar they earn. To paraphrase Spencer Tracy, their pants are so thin they could sit on a coin and tell if it was heads or tails.

If time and money were the same, people would be as generous with one as they are with the other. The opposite, however, is true. People are usually predisposed towards one of the two. Let's take charity as an example. Some people prefer to make regular financial donations to their favourite charitable organisation (money), while others are happier volunteering and helping out (time). It's quite rare for an individual to dedicate energies to both. The same applies to housework. Some people prefer to outsource the cleaning and gardening to hired help (money), while others are happier knowing they've personally maintained the upkeep of their abode (time). Again, it's quite rare to find a person with a strong inclination to take on both.

Personally, I'm a money guy. Even when I don't have any money, I'm still a money guy. Even during the occasions when I've experienced torturous financial strain, when I was desperately cutting costs just to survive, I had sold my house, sold my car, sold my lounge, cancelled my gym membership and stopped all my insurances, all before finally deciding it was probably a good idea to also cancel the cleaner who came in once a week for an hour to tidy the place up. It has been by far the hardest financial decision I've ever made.

The ultimate definition of 'time is money, money is time' is that time is a valuable resource, so make it as productive as possible. You can interpret the word 'productive' in any way that suits. Maybe to you that does mean money. To another it might mean social engagements. To someone else it could be the number of books they read, or movies they see, or relationships they cherish or adventures they experience. Whatever it is, the problem with this cliché is it jumps to the premature evaluation money should be the measure of life. But unlike centimetres, which measure height, and kilograms, which measure weight, money doesn't fit the variety of variables visible in everyday living. Time and money do not correlate. They're about as related as Dick Cheney and North Korea's Kim Jong-il.

People who passionately follow this cliché live hectic lives. They're fast talkers and stormy walkers. They're abrupt and they'll disrupt any sign of empty waffle. Every conversation has a purpose and every meeting has an outcome and heaven help you if you get in the way of their efficiency. They race up escalators like there's a bag of money waiting for them at the claws as they alight. They frantically press the button in elevators in the panicked hope it'll get them to their destination a few seconds sooner. At pedestrian crossings, they don't press the button at all as they madly manoeuvre their way through manic traffic. They rush from one place to another, frightened they'll waste a single minute of their time, conscious of maximising every hour of productivity, without realising that by thinking of their time as money they're wasting the very time they're trying to preserve.

Chapter 31

Focus on the bottom line

It's important to begin this chapter with praise for the bottom line. It's paid my bills, cured my ills and financed my thrills. For a while in my business, it didn't exist. It was like a long-lost lover who never called but would occasionally pop by to pay me a visit, give me a taste of what I'd been missing, and then depart without saying goodbye, leaving me feeling used but glad for the company. After a year of being an on-again off-again couple, we began to understand each other a little better, and especially the things that would make us see red. Then one day the bottom line moved in, and since then we've been inseparable. So, no, I don't begrudge it. What this chapter is about is not what's wrong with this cliché, but what's amiss with how it's being used in the corporate world. Managers who dive into the bottomless pit of management clichés focus excessively on the bottom line like a born-again Christian quoting John 3:16: 'For the Boss so loved the company, that he gave his only begotten cliché, that whosoever believeth in the bottom line should not perish, but have an everlasting career.'

When, as a manager, you have a catchphrase you repeat more frequently than any other, you become known for it among your employees. They associate you with the meaning they place on that sentence and subconsciously attune their attention towards it. I had a manager who would occasionally turn up to meetings later than the appointed time, like we'd all do occasionally. But unlike the rest of us who'd apologise for being late when we entered the room, this manager preferred to sing, 'Apologies, everyone. I'm running behind schedule'. And that seemed to be okay with her because when others would be late for a meeting and they'd say something like 'Sorry, I'm late' she would always scold them by saying in her angry and I'm-too-important-for-this voice, 'CLM, James, C-L-M'. (CLM stood for 'career-limiting move'.)

Eventually we all picked up that, given a choice, she would rather we were behind schedule than late. So one day when I was the one running tragically late for a meeting, I raced across the department floor, rushed up to the meeting room and opened the door, and as I flew in and took my seat, between my out-of-breath pant and her look-of-death slant, I chimed, 'Apologies, everyone. I'm running behind schedule'. If looks could kill, she would have fixed her stare on me and watched me die slowly. With a retort that encompassed both a snort and a growl, she barked, 'You're NOT behind schedule. You're just plain late!' I was confused, because up until then I thought it was acceptable to be behind schedule. So here's where the bottom line comes in. If you talk about it too much where it becomes the centre of your focus to the neglect of other important aspects of business, eventually those employed by you will think that performance really is all about the bottom line and nothing else. They might forsake what's ethical for a slice of bigger profits. They might skimp on quality to save a few dollars. Perhaps they'd abandon sound strategic solutions for short-term gain. Many negative consequences are possible if what you're communicating above and beyond all else is the maximisation of the bottom line.

So if you're going to focus on additional areas on an equal footing with the bottom line, the only element on par with a shareholder's return on their monetary investment is the *front line*, which is a stakeholder's return on their energy investment. And these front-line inputs can be summarised by one word: *relationships*. The most pertinent of all front-line relationships are those you have, not with your customers, but with your staff. Your customers, while they're without doubt an important stakeholder relationship, will be delighted when they're looked after by employees who are full of joy and love for their work, their colleagues, their boss and their company.

When I was 16 I worked as a waiter at a trendy function centre where the owner had such a disproportional focus on the bottom line, that he'd stupidly have very little care for his staff. For example, he didn't even know my age. If he did, he would have realised that I was way too young to be legally serving alcohol in his establishment. As a result, we'd react to the harsh treatment. I would recklessly screw up orders and dizzily drop plates. A colleague, so sulky he had a chip on both shoulders, would steal food and drinks to take home to his family. Another coworker, who had the lowest possible standards and would even fail to achieve those, would revoltingly spit on patrons' foods. And I'm convinced all of that happened because our boss was the kind of person who wanted to squeeze as much as he could out of his personnel so he could bump up his already pumped-up bottom line. (By the way, never be rude to a waiter.)

Sometimes the bottom line isn't the last line of defence. There are certain industries barely making a profit any more such as newspapers. Since readership and advertising revenues have plunged in recent years, newspapers from all around the world have folded, while others have had their profitability ripped to shreds. An economist's argument might be that an unprofitable newspaper should be left to wither away since the demand just isn't there. But that leaves behind a crucial gap in investigative journalism, public education and the exposé of political sex scandals. You might consider the newspaper industry to be as unwanted as a misplaced apostrophe annoying those clever enough to see through its biases, frustrating those too dumb to understand its importance and ruining an otherwise perfect landscape of well-spelt words. Regardless, in some cases, the good a company does for the world is of greater significance than its bottom line, and newspapers fundamentally have a vital role to play in our society. Likewise, other struggling but hugely essential industries shouldn't be shredded because of their profitability, or lack thereof.

There are various causes for the global financial crisis, one of which has been an excessive focus on maximising profits resulting in unethical behaviour. For example, such an unhealthy obsession with the bottom line is what caused lenders to lend to those who shouldn't be taking out a DVD let alone a home loan. So when is enough, enough? It's no longer sufficient for companies to be making a profit; they need to be increasing it each year. But how is it possible for never-ending growth to occur? Surely the earth's capacity for such growth will eventually be reached. What then? What if governments were to make it illegal for an organisation to make a profit? All excess funds would need to be reinvested back into the community. Would that be a good thing, or a bad thing? I have no idea. I don't know the answers to any of these questions and I'm not advocating them as solutions. I'm just thinking aloud; just being curious; just exploring the concept of the bottom line. As they say in the 'hood, perhaps it's 'Not all dat'. The world might be a better place if it didn't exist. (Not the 'hood. The bottom line.) I do love it, though. I'm a capitalist. But there's nothing wrong with questioning the established. There's nothing wrong with rethinking what we think, even if just for a minute. What if we're mistaken about this whole thing and companies aren't meant to be profit-making machines? Is that socialism? I'm not sure. Maybe, just maybe, the bottom line isn't what it's cracked up to be.

Accounting and economics were never my strongest subjects. At high school I was pulled out of class and asked by the mathematics head teacher to give him just one reason why I shouldn't be expelled. Unfortunately, I couldn't give him one. So I'm relying on the experts here when I put it to you that according to many accountants, the bottom line shouldn't be a business's most pressing financial consideration. It's less about profits and more about cash flow. While a business is cash flow positive, it's almost impossible to go broke, whereas a profitable business can still go under at the slightest hiccup. But I understand it's easier to dish out company bonuses based on profit targets than it is to base them on a statement of cash flows. All I'm saying is this is just one more crack in the claim profitability is the be-all and end-all of business success.

The bottom line is the bottom line might not be the bottom line.

Chapter 32

There's no money in the budget

When I quit the corporate world to start my own business, I spent more than a year on Struggle Street. I wasn't just down-and-out. I was way-down-and-far-out. It's not that there wasn't enough money in my budget. It's that there wasn't even *a* budget. For most of the time, I survived on cheese and crackers — sometimes not even cheese; just crackers. I would visit potential clients by jumping the gates at the train station because I couldn't afford to pay for the ticket. There were occasions when I'd travel interstate to speak at a conference but could only purchase a one-way fare, leaving me stranded at the airport, often in a strange town, overnight, until I could somehow scramble the funds together to get back home. I was evicted from my home and afflicted by the insidiousness of not having any money. I've spent a lot of time in India, so I'm aware that what I went through doesn't even compare to what real poverty is like. But it does make me wary when corporate people say there isn't any money in the budget, because that claim is about as truthful as a British MP's expenses declaration.

A while ago, I received an email from one of the world's largest funds-management companies asking me if I'd like to run a workshop for their entire leadership team. 'Fabulous,' I said, 'here's my price.' 'Oh no,' was the reply, 'we don't want to pay you!' They wanted me to train their leaders for free and the only carrot they could provide was that this 'might' lead to further paid work down the track. Let me put it in perspective. Last year, this company made a profit of over $300 million. And that's in Australia alone. My profit in the past year was less than 0.5 per cent of that amount. A lot less. And *they* wanted *me* to give them something for free. Unbelievable. I should have called their helpdesk to ask them for free superannuation. Upon hearing hesitation in their voice, I'd offer them the chance of paid work in the future. I wonder if that would work.

Their excuse for suggesting such an absurd offer was that they didn't have the budget to pay for external providers. With a profit of $300 million, they didn't have the budget? I'm quite a non-confrontational person (despite the tone I use throughout this book), and so I politely declined. If they really cared about their leaders' development, they could have found the money by making cuts elsewhere. Their expenses during that period were about $400 million. Surely somewhere among that expenditure there was room for a small additional cost, which when divided among all of their leaders becomes a tiny investment per person. If they cut the crap as much as they cut the budget, they wouldn't need to ask for free help from small business owners.

Even though an organisation might be making a huge profit, I recognise that the proportion of the budget allocated to each department is tighter than Shania Twain's jeans. But sometimes you don't need to pay in cash if you've got something of value to exchange with the seller. Some of the stuff I've received at no cost includes websites, banners, designs, accommodation, printing and video recording. I just had to provide something of equal value in return. Airline companies can never complain about not having enough money in the budget when there are plenty of providers happy to receive frequent flyer points or club memberships instead. The same deal applies with hotel chains, restaurants, clothing retailers, department stores and electronics outlets, and most types of other businesses, which can similarly pay using their product or service rather than cash, and yes, it'll still cost a little, but it won't whittle away as much of the budget as it otherwise would.

A pushy salesman once tried to sell me an exorbitantly priced service I couldn't afford. I made it clear there was a greater chance of me becoming the First Lady of Uzbekistan than there was of me getting that amount of money. It was a physical impossibility. His response was one I'll never forget. He said, 'Mate, if you found out today that the person you love most in the world had an illness that meant they'd die unless you were able to pay for their life-saving operation, would you find a way of raising the money or not?' Of course, my answer was yes. Mind you, I still didn't buy what he was selling, but I got the lesson — if you want something bad enough, you'll find a way of getting it. It comes down to asking the right question. When we look at spending money within a business, we tend to ask questions such as, '*Do* I have the money for this?' or '*Can* I afford it?' Starting questions with the words 'do' or 'can' are more likely to lead to an answer of 'no' because it's the easy way out. A more helpful question is one that begins with the word 'how', such as 'How can I afford it?' and 'How can I get the money to make this happen?' It transforms you from being remorseful to being resourceful.

Those who base their financial decisions just on whether there's money available in the budget end up neglecting the *real monetary value* of their decisions. This value can be determined by calculating two algorithms. Firstly, what's the cost of *not* going ahead? And secondly, what's the *benefit* of going ahead? If the cost of not proceeding is larger than the size of the investment, then it's reasonable to find the money somehow. And if the gains made by giving the green light bring more advantages than the dollars being spent, then it's logical to find a way to make it happen. The narrow and harrowing view of looking at the budget only as it is today and using that as the sole mechanism for making a financial decision makes about as much sense as a sub-prime loan. It's the equivalent of being held at ransom by a kidnapper, and despite having your phone with you, you don't call anyone for help because you've already reached your monthly cap, and plus, any calls made after 9 pm are charged at 30 cents a minute. There's just no money in the budget.

Let's assume there's no way around the constriction of a fractious budget. It's a feeling akin to being stuck in your car, double-parked. You want to get out but you're blocked and locked in a tight space by the immovable vehicles of debits and the bumper bars of habits. Habits so ingrained that if the budget says no, well then, the budget says no. If that's the case, before scrapping or capping an idea or an initiative, seek an alternative that costs less or costs nothing. Instead of outsourcing training, you might run it yourself. Instead of purchasing new chairs, you might get some donated. Instead of buying biscuits for the tea room, you might steal some from a hospital ward.

Beware of budget smugglers.

Chapter 33

Do what you love and the money will follow

Awards shows are the perfect way to play bingo. On a blank sheet of paper, write down the number of times you expect celebrities in their acceptance speeches to (a) thank God, (b) cry and (c) tell their fans that if they believe, really truly believe in themselves, they too can achieve anything. Then as each predictable incident occurs, cross it off your list. It's a handy way of staying awake once you've endured the banality of the red carpet interviews, where celebrities are asked fundamentally important life questions such as which designer brand they've got draped over their bony shoulders. I can handle the public display of God worship. And the crying is always good for a laugh. But it's the last part that rankles. The 'If I can do it, so can you' line is flawed because it unfairly raises the hopes of millions of wannabes who aspire to be up on that stage wearing jewellery that weighs more than their size zero frame. There's only so much room in the world for A-grade celebrities, both in terms of roles available and space for their egos. Even if all of them believed with every fibre of their bodies they will be award-winning actors, it's outrageous to think even 0.1 per cent of them will succeed in making their dreams come true. Just because they're doing something they love doesn't mean success will follow. The 'Do what you love and the money will follow' cliché and its various derivatives can't explain why there are so many starving artists in the world unable to make a buck, let alone a fortune.

There has to be more to it. It's a little something called 'luck'. Some people are lucky enough to have the stamina to persevere no matter what. Others are lucky enough to have the financial backing of a cashed-up parent. Some are lucky enough to avoid life's goal-diversion catastrophes. Others are lucky enough to have the right talent, or possess the right look, or meet the right person, or get the right education, or be raised in the right country, or be brought up in the right way, or be blessed with the right wisdom and countless other fortunate factors that determine whether or not individuals have what it takes to make money by doing what they love. We're all aware of those who, despite horrible adversity and a total lack of luck, were able to become huge successes, but they're the exceptions. Luck has as much of a role to play in financial success as love of the work. This isn't me justifying the triumphs of those I dislike while ignoring Earl Wilson when he said, 'Success is simply a matter of luck. Ask any failure'. What this is about is an acknowledgement that, whether big or small, good luck is a factor in people's financial success, and bad luck is a factor in people's financial failures.

There are some jobs where it's inconceivable to make a lot of money irrespective of how much you love them. Take library assistants, for example. They often do what they do because they love reading books. They'd be hard-pressed turning that into a million-dollar idea. Then there are underpaid professions like nursing. I've got a friend who works as a nurse because there's no other job in the world he'd rather do, but he's had to accept he'll need to marry money or inherit it if he's ever going to be wealthy. Add to the list social workers, childcare workers, hairdressers, musicians and other occupations that leave a savings account unoccupied and you'll start to see that money hasn't followed the millions of people who've chosen a career based solely on what they love.

I guess you could turn this around and say a library assistant could write a book, but that's ignoring the fact that reading a book and writing one are two separate skills. You could say a hairdresser could open up her own salon, but that's assuming someone who loves doing perms will have an aptitude for managing staff and account keeping. Just because some people have succeeded at making money from their passion doesn't mean everyone can. Let's add to the mix what most people love are usually hobbies and other recreational interests, and the fallacy behind 'Do what you love and the money will follow' becomes more obvious. Personally, I love playing the brick-breaker game on my BlackBerry, watching re-runs of *Melrose Place* and writing in lead pencils. If I should ever start making large amounts of money from these activities, I'll give you a refund on this book. Unless you're able to turn your favourite pastime into something that's commercial, something people will happily pay for, then for 99 per cent of us, the money simply will not follow.

It's true you could get more enjoyment from life by doing work you love. For most of us, this means putting up with not earning as much as we'd like. On the flip side, there are people earning obscene amounts of money but who hate their jobs with about as much fervour as they spend. You would've seen servers at fast-food outlets earning $10 an hour but with beaming smiles that could melt the faces off Mount Rushmore. And then you would've seen high-powered executives earning $10 000 an hour but with sneers that could turn it into Mount Uproar. These two cases show the cause and no-effect relationship between love and money. If money follows love it's usually not because of love but due to other reasons we disregard in favour of the more romantic notion of cash-inducing job satisfaction. If anything, it's the opposite of this cliché that's more often accurate. It's not that money follows what you love, but having money gives you greater opportunities to do what you love.

That's why so many of us are addicted to the drastic-plastic credit cards. We so badly want the chance to do what we love that we finance it by going into easy debt. There was a point in my life where my credit card debt was the horrendous sum of $50 000. Still desperate to get my hands on more cash to fund the lifestyle and activities to which I'd become accustomed, I called one of the big banks to request a fourth credit card. Not only did they approve my application, but the representative said, 'James, I can see that the credit cards you have with us are already over-limit and that you haven't paid your minimum payments for the past three months … but I'll just pretend I didn't see that'. Great. And I pretended I could pay them back.

It's unrealistic to create dream jobs for most of your employees. The way to amplify job satisfaction is to incorporate their natural talents into their work. This doesn't mean their jobs *become* their talents; just at some stage during the week, they're able to utilise their talents in the work that they do. That's when they'll grow to love their jobs. It's a bit like marrying someone for money but then realising afterwards his heart is even deeper than his wallet, or her mind is even more open than her purse. For many people, love is stronger when their financial needs are met up-front whether it's in their personal lives or at work.

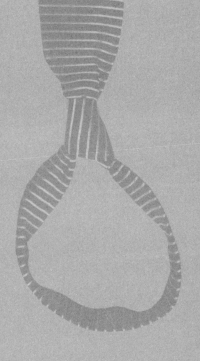

Part IX

All's fair in love and work

Chapter 34

It's not what you know, it's who you know

I'd rather give birth to an elephant than go to a networking function — and that's coming from an extrovert. There's not much to like about them, really. For starters, there are the superficial conversations far more boring than even parents talking about their kids, and if you think that the 'So, do you come here often?' line is reserved for smoky bars, think again. At networking events, that line's used as an awkward silence filler when the only other alternative is to challenge them to a staring competition to see who'll blink first. Then there are the pushy sellers with over-eager egos shoving business cards in your hand like they're going out of fashion, trying to get around to as many people as possible to maximise their contacts. And of course, my personal favourite, the perennial question: 'So what do you do?' That one sends a chill down my spine every time. It's blaringly obvious that the folk flapping around at these events are fervent followers of this cliché. By thinking 'It's not what you know, it's who you know' they're cutting themselves off from what they actually need to know. In this chapter, I provide you with five alternatives to this exhausted cliché that just wants some time alone.

It's not who you know, but to whom you're connected

I'm on Facebook. Not on Twitter, just on Facebook. When it comes to Twitter, I agree with one of my favourite columnists, Maureen Dowd, who said, 'I would rather be tied up to stakes in the Kalahari Desert, have honey poured over me and red ants eat out my eyes than open a Twitter account'. But back to Facebook. If you're on there, I'm sure you've got friends who amass stacks of 'friends'. I've got contacts who have thousands of people on their friends list, almost all of whom they do not know. These shallow and shadowy friendships mean nothing. If anything, they could be trouble as the profile owner's private details are exposed for all to gawk at. Business card collectors do a similar thing. Firm believers that their businesses will grow the more people they know, they hoard these pieces of cardboard as if they're nuggets of gold. They don't realise it's not the quantity of people on your database, but the connection you have with them that's important. Just because you 'know' 1000 people doesn't mean that they'll do anything for you in the future. But the ones you meaningfully cultivate a relationship with will at least be receptive to the idea. It's not about knowing, but about bonding.

It's not who you know, but who knows you

Far more powerful than a collection of names you've got stored on a spreadsheet are the people that have your name stored in their minds. It's the difference between pushing yourself onto people and pulling them in towards you. When I first started my business, I was a pusher. I'd attend the networking events, I'd make the cold-blooded cold calls and I'd send the promotional packs. It was such a degrading and soul-destroying way to do business. I'd walk into a meeting reeking of desperation, with my body language and tone screaming to the buyer: 'Book me, damn you! *Book me!*' Needless to say, but I'll say it anyway, potential clients would look at me with a look on their face as if I'd just told them I was on parole, then they'd boot me out of their office faster than a fully sick driver. And despite leaving up to seven voicemails per client over the subsequent weeks, none would ever be returned.

After a year of rejection and dejection, I changed my tactic to one of pulling rather than pushing, and the results were much better. Instead of forcing myself onto potential clients, I was attracting them towards me via articles, newsletters, books and other means that slowly created a following. I stopped caring about the number of people I knew, and started caring about the number of people that knew me, and that was when I began to love my work.

It's not who you know, but what you do

So you've got a big database. So what? It's what you do with the people you know that determines how fast you grow. The frequency of contact and the quality of that contact are paramount. One of my oratory idols is Australia's most successful broadcaster, Alan Jones. Despite what you think of his political views, there's no denying the man is a masterful wordsmith, an outstanding communicator and a commanding influencer.

When I was in my early 20s, I had the pleasure of meeting Alan at the commercial radio industry awards, where I was helping out a friend who had organised the event. I was assigned the task of being Alan's chaperone. In talking to Alan at the event, I subtly slipped into the conversation my desire to someday be a radio broadcaster, and with the generosity he's famous for, Alan kindly gave me his mobile number and invited me to spend time with him in the studio. I was happier than a bee with a bum full of honey. Here I was with a radio god's personal phone number, rapport already built and a willingness to lend a hand. I was so overwhelmed with my good fortune... that I did nothing with it. In the weeks that followed, I was so anxious to impress him that I couldn't bring myself to call. More nervous than a nurse with a full bedpan, I would flood and torment my head with thoughts and counter-thoughts of the best way to get in contact with him, and what I would say and how I would say it and before I knew it over a month had gone by and still not a peep left my lips. By this time I was convinced he'd forgotten me already, so I decided to send him a letter since I'd heard through a friend that Alan Jones 'loves' letters. He never replied to the postal correspondence and I never had the backbone to pick up the phone. Till this day it haunts me as one of my biggest regrets, but it reinforced in me the distinction between who I know and what I do with the people I know.

It's not who you know, but who you are

If people with whom you do business could use just one word to describe you, what would it be? When thinking of the answer, don't ponder what you'd *like* the word to be, but what that word actually *is*, because the number of people you know isn't a turn-on if the person you are is a turn-off. I know a guy who attends every networking event. It seems as though he's miraculously able to be in two or three places at the one time, that's how often he pops up at these gatherings. Yet there's something sinister, slimy and insincere about him. If he were to talk to you, he'd make your skin crawl like some kind of flesh-eating bacteria making its way across your body. It's a combination of the clothes he wears, his unkempt exterior, his negative disposition, the way he pounces on you if he thinks you're a VIP and a host of other features that paint him as an out-of-touch untouchable. He snatches business cards from anyone (or anything) with a pulse (or without), and expects this to result in more business success. If you were to count his business cards and LinkedIn connections, you'd assume he knows thousands upon thousands of people. But because of who he is, he really knows no-one.

It's not what you know, but how you use it

Smart people do a lot of dumb things. From public figures cheating on their spouses to financial whiz-kids rorting the system, people with lots of brains but not enough brakes can't stop themselves from falling down. Perhaps they slip up because of that very reason. They're clever. They know so much about something or some things that their scheming mind wanders to what's seemingly possible even if it's illegal or immoral. How they use what they know is what in the end brings them undone. When I used to work in the corporate world, there was an occasion where I applied for a promotion which involved completing one of those five-hour psychometric examinations. When the psychologist called me to give me the results, in a clinical and clammy tone, her feedback went a little something like this: 'Numeracy test — below average. Logic test — below average. Social test — below average. And vocabulary test — below average. But don't worry, because out of everyone in the below-average category, you came out on top'. So basically, what she was saying was that out of all the losers, I was the biggest loser. With results like those, I didn't get the promotion. The job went to a deadbeat who passed the tests but flunked in the role because it wasn't what he knew that mattered, but how he used it.

The phrase 'Don't you know who I am?' has never had more relevance.

Chapter 35

Treat people how you'd like to be treated

I'm glad I don't stick to this strict edict. Actually, I think everyone else is glad, too. Let's imagine what life would be like if I treated others in the way I like to be treated. For starters, I would avoid all conversations with acquaintances since I find few exchanges as dreary as the ones about my day — and, to be frank, theirs. I would also buy Greek CDs for all of my friends and colleagues — even when they speak about as much Greek as they do Klingon. And I would make sure that all client meetings were held in my home during the commercial breaks of *The Bold and the Beautiful*, because I love talking about business in among a discussion on whether Ridge should be with Brooke or with Taylor. This cliché, otherwise known as The Golden Rule, should really be called The Olden Rule, because what worked during the biblical era doesn't work today where the people we interact with are more diverse than ever before.

It's impractical and unrealistic to impose our preferences on others, so a more fitting fit-out of this cliché to suit these modern times would be: treat others how *they* would like to be treated. This means if someone's an extrovert I'll ramp up my gregariousness, but I'll soften it when they're an introvert. If a friend simply wants me to listen to her dilemmas, then I won't try to solve them like a wannabe Agony Aunt. I learnt this lesson very early in my career when I was fortunate enough to land several training engagements in Dubai. With nought for thought, I delivered a program similar to what I'd ordinarily do in Australia, and it flopped. It just never occurred to me an Islamic audience would respond unfavourably towards jokes about alcohol, internet dating and sex. In my mind, I was treating them how I like to be treated in training programs, but the result is that the invoice I sent them is still outstanding all these years later. (Note to self: send them a payment reminder notice.)

Each individual has a preferred method of communicating which comes naturally to them. It's often done without thinking. A trap that people fall into when they abide by the 'treat others how you'd like to be treated' cliché is they communicate using their own default style. Their autopilot switches on and unless the person with whom they're communicating shares the same preference as them, they struggle to get the recipient's attention. As Margaret Miller once quipped, 'Most conversations are simply monologues delivered in the presence of a witness' which gives a whole new meaning to the term 'witness protection program'. What they need protecting from is the verbal gunfire shot from the mouths of people who don't cater their communication style to suit the audience. This is especially important for leaders where your ability to influence the individual members of your team is determined by how flexible you are in triggering their senses. This means being to-the-point with direct employees, using stories and emotion with expressive employees, incorporating data and facts with analytical employees and being calm and inclusive with amiable employees.

But that's just communication. What about motivation? The proponents of 'treat people how you'd like to be treated' motivate their staff in the same way they personally get motivated. The result ends up being a one-size-fits-all policy that really fits no-one. It becomes a one-prize-shits-all policy. As devised by the University of Rochester, there are seven forms of intrinsic motivation. Depending on how big your team is, you might need to find a way of using all of these while you're at work to get the best from your team: *challenge*—where people want their skills stretched; *curiosity*—for employees who want to experience something new that arouses their attention; *control*—when they want more autonomy over what happens at work; *fantasy*—the use of imagination and games to stimulate learning; *competition*—for people who like comparing their performance to others; *cooperation*—for employees who value relationships above all else; and *recognition*—the innate desire to be acknowledged and appreciated. People are generally driven by just one or two of these. Using only your personal preference (that is, how you like to be treated) motivates the few people in your team who are just like you, but leaves everyone else about as motivated as a pregnant cow.

Since people have different styles of communication, motivation, learning and working, your challenge is to find out these preferences for each employee, colleague, manager and anybody else with whom you choose to interact. The only way to do this is by asking and telling. You ask your employees how they'd like to be managed and you tell your boss how you'd like to be managed. Ditto with communication and the others.

I once ran a team-building day with a group of leaders who hated each other. If murder wasn't illegal, it's safe to assume there'd be only one of them still breathing. I thought it'd be a good idea to start the day by getting the participants to share with the group something about their personal lives that no-one knew. When it was a quaint and quiet lady's turn, she said in a soft voice, 'Something personal about my life is that I hate being touched. I don't know why, I just hate it. I always have. I never want to shake your hand and I never want you to hug me. It gives me the creeps. So, don't touch me and we'll get along just fine'. At that moment, one of the men sitting on the other side of the boardroom stood up, walked over to where this lady sat and, to our absolute horror, placed his hands all over her body as if he was frisking her for a concealed weapon. In his mind, this was an innocent action that would make everyone laugh. No-one laughed. But she erupted. She pushed her chair away and ran out of the room, leaving me thinking what a perfect start to the team-building day this had been. 'Okay then, who's next?' I ding-donged hopefully. They looked at me as if I'd asked them to go out and rob graves.

The only place for 'treat people how you'd like to be treated' is in primary school. It's a wonderful lesson to teach kids, since this simplistic cliché can teach them about empathy and reciprocity. But once kids become teenagers, where as adolescents they start to learn about influence and persuasiveness, it becomes like a trick-or-treat activity where to treat others how they'd like to be treated is the only way to avoid being tricked.

Chapter 36

Coming up with a win-win solution

Hailed as a panacea for workplace ills, the win-win solution teaches mediators how to get warring parties happily agreeing to a solution, but what it ignores is that our society is unbreakably built around the concept of win-lose. The way we avidly follow sport is driven by our desire to see our favourite team trump the competition, not to negotiate an outcome with them. Our political system has at its core an uncompromising principle to attack the opposition, since winning an election is more important than collaboration. From winning a university place to winning the heart of a potential lover, and from being the prettiest to being the richest, our society thrives on competition where someone ends up being better than the other. This was exemplified by Ray Kroc, the guy who built McDonald's into one of the world's most formidable brands, when he said, 'If any of my competitors were drowning, I'd stick a hose in their mouth'.

Anyone who's attended training on conflict resolution would have encountered this conflicting cliché. There's a very funny scene in the American version of *The Office*, which showcases the irrationality of win-win. In the episode, two employees are in conflict over a poster on a wall. One employee, Angela, wants it up, while the other, Oscar, wants it taken down. So Michael, the manager, decides to resolve the conflict by consulting his mediation handbook. He begins by seeing if the employees are aware of the five different forms of conflict, the first one being lose-lose, where no-one gets what they want. He then flicks through the folder and announces that win-win is number four while win-win-win is number five. Strictly adhering to the handbook, Michael asks Oscar and Angela to describe how they feel about the poster using 'I' emotion language, no judging and no 'You' statements. When that tactic fails, he resorts to brainstorming. When that also fails, Michael decides Angela should turn the poster into a T-shirt Oscar wears, that way Oscar doesn't have to see it but Angela can still look at it whenever she glances his way. The two of them object, at which point a colleague suggests the poster be up on Tuesdays and Thursdays. Michael disagrees, since that's a 'compromise', which is only number three in the handbook. Confident that his T-shirt idea is a win-win, Michael demands this be the solution, leaving Angela reeling like Angel Eyes, who was 'the bad' in *The Good, The Bad, and The Ugly*, and Oscar with the temperament of Oscar the Grouch. No-one was happy. No-one had won.

Here's the irony. People who aim for a win-win solution do so because they're taught 'compromise' as an option is imperfect. Yet more often than not, win-win solutions are in effect compromises anyway since it's virtually impossible for both parties to get exactly what they want. If we look at the scene from *The Office*, Michael's win-win solution resulted in Angela having to see the poster on Oscar's body rather than the wall, while Oscar had to put up with having an image on his body that he regarded as 'more offensive than hard-core porn'. What complemented the win-win was a compromise.

When it comes to workplace conflict, it's hard to keep everyone satisfied with the outcome. I remember two sweet and lovely young women in my team who turned conflict, the noun, into inflict — the verb. They began with verbal assaults, but when that got boring they would threaten each other with stabbings, strangulations, bashings and on two occasions they engaged in fist-fighting and hair-pulling. They must have misinterpreted me when I encouraged them to 'beat each other'. I was referring to a team competition, not a boxing ring. We tried the win-win approach which led nowhere, so we made a decision that benefited one of them more than the other. This wasn't because someone had to win or lose, but because one employee was in the right more so than her opponent. It wasn't the ideal textbook-favoured option to adopt, but it dealt with the problem well enough for us to move on. Sometimes it's better to settle for a compromise that's close enough to the romantic notion of a win-win scenario, than to strive for the idealistic and unrealistic hopes of having everyone's wishes granted.

If you have the time and energy available, the win-win solution might work for you occasionally. Just be prepared for a drawn-out and painstaking process. What you'll find is that it's only feasible when consensus is absolutely necessary, which isn't the case for every decision, or for every conflict, or for every change of plan. In the majority of cases, it's likely there'll be a winner and a loser. Mary Ashton Livermore broke a well-known cliché back in the 1800s when she joked, 'Whoever said, "It's not whether you win or lose that counts" probably lost'. It matters when people lose, and so long as you're there to provide support to those who missed out on getting what they want, then you're doing your job. Effective management isn't about getting your employees to always agree with you, but it is about getting them to always understand. When they comprehend the rationale behind your decisions, and they know it's come from an intention that genuinely means well, they'll accept that everything won't always go their way.

What the win-win solution ignores is that some people are motivated intensely by competition. It's what drives them, sets them alight and makes them contribute their best at work. If you were to implement a win-win solution as much as possible, you'd deny a large group of employees what they need to be engaged. Negotiation is not important to these people. In many cases, neither is collaboration. They just want to win, and to win by a mile.

I see it in yoga all the time. There are two types of people who go to yoga classes. There are those of us who do it as much for the spiritual benefits as we do for the physical exercise. We perform the poses using perfect posture, we breathe the way that we're instructed, and we really get into the 'om' chanting. But then there are 'the others'. These are the people who attend yoga just to show off. They're fiercely competitive. They want to be the best and they want you to know it. They don't tolerate anyone else going further in a pose, so you can bet they'll go deeper than you even if they have to dislocate their shoulder to do it. They're competitive in every aspect of their lives, but we need them. Competition creates better products, enhanced services and motivated employees. The win-win solution ignores these people.

With a win-win solution, you'll win some and lose some, despite what the textbooks tell you.

Chapter 37

Having an open-door policy

With a lot of the clichés in this book, it's actually the opposite that's the truth. Not so with this one. Imagine what it would be like if a company espoused and promoted a closed-door policy to its employees. 'At Big Bank, your thoughts are not important to us. If you feel the urge to submit an idea, please place it in the suggestion box which we will collect once a year for recycling purposes. For any brand management issues such as harassment claims, bullying incidents or whistleblower enquiries, please visit public relations immediately. For all other complaints, see HR who will attend to your problem as soon as they've redesigned the appraisal system for the third time this month. And for any other general enquiries, let's take those offline.' Hmmm, I don't think so. A closed-door policy just wouldn't work, and yet there's still so much about the open-door policy that's not quite right. It's a creaky and rusty old thing.

It's always intrigued me that the proudest managers who shout the loudest about their open-door policy are usually those who'd like it slammed shut the most. They falter because they take the words in this cliché *literally*. They interpret them as meaning 'leave the office door open', but that's not what the open-door policy is about. The real intention of it is for managers to be *accessible* and *approachable*. A manager's door might be wide open and yet he could be the antithesis of this cliché, while another manager might have the door firmly locked yet truly be what this cliché represents.

I had a new boss who really wanted to make an impression on her first day so she decided to give up her office altogether. She wanted to 'sit among the people'. So she turned her office into a meeting room and grabbed a desk near us. We were stunned. The chatter on the department floor was centred on how amazing this new manager was for relinquishing the prestige of having an office just so she could be closer to her employees. How thoughtful! How generous! How admirable! How totally and utterly... repugnant. She was a vulture. Giving up her office was just a token gesture to disguise she had people skills on par with Chucky. She'd sit at her desk for hours with her back hunched over, a stern and scrunched up look on her face, her entire attention fixed on the computer screen and her short stubby fingers banging away at the keyboard furiously. If any of us even dared to approach her den, she'd snarl without looking up from her screen with a vicious, *'Not now!'* Her open-door policy was so open she had no door, and yet we would have preferred Chucky.

What's far more important than an open-door policy is an open-mind policy. Let's assume you're accessible and approachable. If you're not receptive to new ideas, there's no point in having an open door policy in the first place. A colleague of mine had a manager who had his door wide open but his mind locked up. No matter who went and saw him with a request, his frazzled response was always the same: 'That's an administrative nightmare!' It was his way of saying 'no' without considering what was being proposed. It was much easier for him to answer everything with the maddened, 'That's an administrative nightmare' than to contemplate (and cater to) his employees' initiatives. If the building was on fire and someone suggested the fire brigade should be called, he'd probably still reply with a bothered, 'That's an administrative nightmare!' In fact, the only nightmare around was him, and was one from which nobody could awaken.

The most excellent managers don't wait for employees to approach them via an open-door policy. Instead, they become proactive listeners. They make a concerted effort to find out what their employees are thinking, feeling, and doing. They go out of their way to bring the open door to the employee rather than the other way around.

A senior executive I used to work with latched onto this idea so he started holding catch-up sessions over lunch. He'd provide sandwiches, and in return, front-line employees would come along, ask questions, air grievances and talk about what's going on 'at the coalface'. This would have worked extremely well had the executive not been the argumentative type. Instead of listening, he would debate. Instead of caring, he would attack. Instead of being helpful, his sessions became a hindrance to the open communication he was trying to foster. People would dread them. They'd return to their desks drained of energy, and in some cases, drained of life. And yet, when he was interviewed in the media, he'd profess the success of his open-door policy and catch-up sessions, when really, he would have been better off without them. He eventually cancelled those lunch gatherings when his assistant noticed the lack of registrations and advised him the caterers don't make food platters for groups of one.

The positive effect of the open-door policy is employees can bypass the corporate hierarchy. The negative effect of the open-door policy is employees can bypass the corporate hierarchy. On the positive side, middle managers and executives get unfiltered feedback from the front-line, and employees get access to important decision-makers. But on the negative side, there are supervisors feeling disheartened the ladder of authority isn't being respected. They might feel the relevance of their role has been diminished since they're no longer the first point of contact for their employees. It's like being refused entry into a nightclub by a bouncer but then announcing smugly that you're friends with the owner. As you walk in with your head held high, ego starts to creep in since you've bypassed security, and you become what Barbara Stanwyck described when she said, 'Egotism is usually just a case of mistaken nonentity'. Meanwhile, the bouncer is left with his head hanging low, his role worth somewhat less in responsibility than it once was. This is not a huge issue, but it is one to keep in mind. The morale of your team leaders is more important than the morale of your employees because there's no way employees will be happy if their bosses are disillusioned.

Whether it's being busy or looking busy, managers have a lot of stuff to do. Okay, *most* managers have a lot of stuff to do. An open-door policy can result in employees constantly barging in, impacting their productivity and forcing them to be available all of the time. It's an unrealistic and unreasonable expectation, one which is unnecessary for the world's best managers. They don't need to have an open-door policy when their pleasant manner and emotional intelligence create environments of free-flowing and honest communication. Naturally. Comfortably. Unforced. Unscripted. Genuinely open.

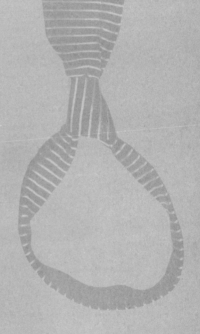

Part X

End a helping hand

Chapter 38

The hit list

The final section of this book is a smash-and-dash look at 10 additional clichés that have contaminated the corridors of the corporate world. As you read through these, you'll recognise yourself as the offender in some and the casualty in others. Either way, please join me in farewelling management clichés forever.

The devil's in the details

For those of us who view attention-to-detail with very little fondness, hearing this cliché makes us shiver at the thought of doing a task for which our brains have not been wired. History repeatedly throws our way examples of the devil not being in the details but in the actual idea. It's not the fine print that's the problem — it's the concept. In 1999 *Time* magazine released its Top 100 Worst Ideas of the Century, as voted by hundreds of thousands of people. Here's some of what made the list: Prohibition, suntans, asbestos, cryogenics, aerosol cheese, infomercials, psychic hotlines and the chain email. If you winced at any of those, it's not because of the detail but because of the idea. That's where the devil lies. Now, on another note, if you forward copies of this book to five people within the next 30 minutes, you'll have good luck for the next year and in a week's time you'll receive a cheque in the mail for $100. It's freaky, but it works. Trust me.

My hands are tied

There's a character named Carol Beer in the *Little Britain* comedy series. She's a chronically unhelpful receptionist, and there's one scene in particular where she's working in a hospital. A mother walks in with her five-year-old daughter and tells Carol her daughter's there to have her tonsils removed. Carol checks her computer and responds with, 'I've got her down for a double hip replacement'. When the mother says there must be some kind of mistake, Carol types away at the keyboard and then retorts with, 'Computer says no'. The mother continues to insist her daughter doesn't need her hips replaced and the response from Carol every time is an uncaring, 'Computer says no'. Exasperated, the mother asks Carol, 'Well, could you speak with somebody?' Carol's reaction is, 'I could, but…' and then shrugs her shoulders with indifference. The scene ends with the mother storming out of the hospital — just after Carol asks her to complete a customer service questionnaire.

Carol is reminiscent of managers who say, 'My hands are tied'. Rather than helping employees by being resourceful, they shrug their shoulders with indifference and say, 'Company says no'. This response is a resignation that results in resignations. It's admitting defeat without having a shot. If bureaucracy gets in the way of doing what you want, keep in mind it's easier to justify your consequences than to seek permission for your actions. In other words, if you really think something is in the best interests of your team and the organisation, just do it anyway. Let the results speak for themselves.

You're only as strong as your weakest employee

If this cliché was accurate, sports teams with weak players wouldn't go on to win grand finals, and yet they do. When a team has players who are strong, they make up for the weak ones. When the strongest are able to carry the rest despite the weak pulling it back, any substance from this cliché is gone. Since I follow sport about as closely as I follow the World Beard and Moustache Championships (they really exist), I can't provide you with specific sporting examples, but I'd like you to imagine leading a team achieving all of its targets, and then having your manager consider your team as underperforming solely because you've got a dud worker who won't pull his weight. It's absurd. This doesn't mean we should ignore the weakest workers, but we shouldn't consider the whole team to be a failure just because of a weak link, either. A piece of fruit might have a bruise or two, but that doesn't mean it can't be eaten.

A fish rots from the head down

Fast Company magazine went on a mission back in 2007 to find out whether or not this phrase was a fact. One of the experts they spoke to was David Groman, a fish pathologist who works in the Atlantic Veterinary College located at the University of Prince Edward Island. He's a specialist in understanding how and why fish die and rot. In the article, Groman responds to the 'fish rots from the head down' cliché by saying, 'It's a poor metaphor. And, I must say, it's biologically incorrect. When a fish rots, the organs in the gut go first'. I trust him, since a large part of his job involves conducting fish autopsies. So even from the outset, this cliché stinks of being incorrect.

In the workplace, there's no denying the negative influence a bad executive could have on the organisation, but the source of all the rot isn't always from the CEO's office. The guts of the organisation, which could be an unethical manager, a corrupt employee, a fraudulent accountant and other greedy souls, all stem from places elsewhere within the business — not only at the top. If the executives deal with it appropriately when it's brought to their attention and they put in place mechanisms to stop it from recurring, then it's a separate kettle of fish. They've done their job. Something smells fishy only when they ignore it like a sign in a pet store saying 'Don't touch the animals'.

Choose a job you love and you'll never work a day in your life

It was Confucius who came up with this hopeful saying that has spread among corporate employees searching for their dream job. I'm not sure what kinds of jobs were around back in 400 BCE, but I can't imagine there'd be many professions that didn't feel like hard work no matter how intensely they were loved. At some stage you would have met someone who's said work doesn't feel like work because they love it so much. They're due for a holiday. Spending a week lying on a Hawaiian beach with a cocktail in hand should be enough to remind even the most obsessive workaholic that work is still work irrespective of how much they adore it. I love what I do immensely. I'm passionate about it. But that doesn't mean I'd prefer to write a book than a travel itinerary. It doesn't mean I'd rather speak to an audience than a hotel porter. And it doesn't mean I'd choose to host a workshop over a pool party. So let's stop lying to ourselves (and others) with this nonsense. Work will always be work. If you happen to love it, then all the better.

Fail to plan, plan to fail

I don't want to denigrate this cliché too much, because it serves its purpose to some extent. Planning helps prepare for the future but the future is so unpredictable. We can't predict what's going to happen in a month let alone in a year—let alone five. Woody Allen is famous for blending humour with the truth. He did this when he said of planning, 'If you want to make God laugh, tell Him your future plans'. If planning too little results in failure, so does planning too much. If you've ever been on a trip with an over-planner, you'll know this to be true. The sparkle of spontaneity is ruled out with their strict schedules. If you've ever put on an event (such as a wedding) with an over-planner, you'll know what I'm talking about. That's when Bridezillas come out to prey. The additional danger is you'll spend so much time in the planning phase you'll never get a chance to get started. You'll always be stuck planning. That's why a book titled *The One Page Business Plan* became a bestseller back in the late 1990s. It acknowledged the value that planning plays in business success, but only in moderation.

Lead, follow or get out of the way

How's that for an ultimatum? Option 1: take charge. Option 2: do as I say. Option 3: move! I agree with the first option. There should always be a leader. But I'm flummoxed by the second. Being a great leader isn't about getting people to follow you just because it's the least painful out of the available choices. It's about getting people to follow you because they're inspired by your vision, or entranced by your style, or motivated by your drive, or stimulated by your intellect, or amazed by your experience or a stack of other possibilities. A reluctant follower is not a follower. You need to give people a reason to follow you otherwise that thing called 'commitment' becomes decommissioned. When you lead people brilliantly, you bring them with you rather than dragging them your way. They come along for the ride rather than being thrown in the boot. To demand someone follows you is the flimsiest way to lead. And as for the third option, there'd be no reason for people to 'get out of the way' if the leadership and followership are done well. It's a redundant option, kinda like your job if the people in your team are about as enthusiastic as Stone Cold Steve Austin playing netball.

Moving forward and going forward

Moving Forward is just as well known as his wife, Going Forward. The Forwards are the most over-invited guests at corporate events. Whether it's a small intimate get-together, such as a coaching session, or a more highbrow affair, such as a business strategy day, you can bet your corner office that the Forwards will be there making their way through the crowd. One thing's for certain — no matter where they go, they're on everyone's lips. No-one's quite sure precisely what value they add to a conversation, but nonetheless, they'll gatecrash every discussion, every long lunch and every big boardroom. They're dismissed as much as they're embraced, and they're disliked as much as they're liked, yet nothing stops them from popping up when you least expect them, drinking from the cups of language and snacking on the canapés of words, until there's nothing left but droplets and morsels of bland corporate-speak. Those who like being a little more creative with how they start their sentences can't stand the Forwards. They long for the day when they're ostracised from corporate society. They yearn for the moment when those who brought the Forwards so willingly into the fold are forced to defend the uselessness of this famous couple. Truth be told, if the Forwards were to die tomorrow, nobody would really miss them. They're like the workmates you promise to stay in touch with after you resign, but of course, never do. It's an awful thing to say, I know, but I think it's the only way to keep the corporate world... moving forward.

Let's take it offline

This is the workplace equivalent of 'shut your pie-hole'. Restricted by cumbersome HR guidelines and blocked by burdensome harassment laws, managers resort to 'let's take it offline' as a way of getting vocal team members to stop talking. There's nothing particularly wrong with this cliché. Some conversations need to be wound up and others are totally irrelevant. According to the *Oxford Dictionary*, there are 171 476 words currently in use in the English language. Somewhere among that vast treasure of syllables, surely you can find something to replace 'Let's take it offline'. And if you're not really a wordsmith and you think you'd struggle, that's fine — use sign language. Place your finger on your lips as if to say, 'Shhhh'. Slide your finger across your throat as if to say, 'One more word and you're dead'. Throw a dart at the talker's head; spray them with a water pistol; grab them in a headlock until they're almost blue (but still breathing). Anything is better than the contagiously insipid disease of talking like everyone else. 'Let's take it offline' might have been a catchy saying the first few times it was used, but now it's old. It's time to take 'Let's take it offline' offline.

At the end of the day

At the end of the day, it's fitting for the final section in this last chapter to focus on another useless cliché that's almost always used to begin a new sentence. At the end of the day, there are a tonne of words that could be used in its place, such as ultimately, eventually and after all. At the end of the day, perhaps it's not even meant to be about replacing this worn-out phrase, but rather, when you get the urge to declare it, use it as an opportunity to take a breath and think. At the end of the day, this cliché is enough to make you sneer at the orator in question with the retort, 'At the end of *which* day in particular?' At the end of the day, there are some things at work that we just don't need, such as staff retreats where you see your boss in his swimsuit; tacky posters with photos of penguins and a headline saying 'Teamwork' and 'Attitude' instead of 'Why bother?' and the way this cliché is endlessly repeated at meeting after meeting.

If you were to go back through that paragraph and remove every time I started a sentence with 'At the end of the day', you'll see it makes no difference to the meaning of each sentence, thereby rendering this cliché meaningless. But its removal does make a difference to the sanity of the person reading it or hearing it. Its days are numbered.

Index

Free newsletter and e-books

Join thousands of managers who receive James's complimentary fortnightly newsletter, which contains helpful tips on how to attract, motivate, engage and retain the best employees. By subscribing you also receive a stack of free e-books (valued at more than $100) on talent management, recruitment, motivation and more. To subscribe simply visit <www.jamesadonis.com> and click on 'With Compliments'.

Management development

James's company, Team Leaders, specialises in the development of front-line managers. The program begins with a one-day workshop, which is followed by monthly face-to-face group mentoring sessions, monthly audio programs, books, newsletters and online forums, so that participants are transformed into extraordinary leaders. For more information visit <www.teamleaders.com.au>.

Business blog

James's blog, Work in Progress, which is nationally syndicated through the Fairfax network, is one of the most commented-on business blogs in the country. It has topics covering every aspect of workplace relations, so check it out and join the conversation. Visit <http://blogs.theage.com.au/small-business/workinprogress/>.